Henry Fielding

Twayne's English Authors Series

Bertram H. Davis, Editor
Florida State University

TEAS 393

HENRY FIELDING
(1707–1754)
Photograph of a sketch by Hogarth,
engraved by James Basire

Henry Fielding

By Richard J. Dircks

St. John's University

Twayne Publishers • Boston

Henry Fielding

Richard J. Dircks

Copyright © 1983 by G.K. Hall & Company
All Rights Reserved
Published by Twayne Publishers
A Division of G. K. Hall & Company
70 Lincoln Street
Boston, Massachusetts 02111

Book Production by Marne B. Sultz

Book Design by Barbara Anderson

Printed on permanent/durable acid-free
paper and bound in the United States of
America.

Library of Congress Cataloging in Publication Data

Dircks, Richard J.
   Henry Fielding.

   (Twayne's English authors series ; TEAS 393)
   Bibliography: p. 132
   Includes index.
   1. Fielding, Henry, 1707–1754—Criticism and
interpretation.
I. Title.   II. Series.
PR3457.D55   1983   823'.5   83-10723
ISBN 0-8057-6768-1

For Phyllis

Contents

About the Author

Richard J. Dircks is Professor of English at St. John's University, New York. He has previously served as Chairman of the English Department, Associate Dean of the Graduate School of Arts and Sciences, and Director of the Humanities Research Center. He received his Ph. D. degree from Fordham University and has taught at Seton Hall University and at Fordham as well as at St. John's.

Professor Dircks, author of *Richard Cumberland* (Twayne 1976), has written on a number of other major eighteenth-century authors, including Jonathan Swift, Oliver Goldsmith, and Samuel Johnson. His work has appeared in leading periodicals, including *Philological Quarterly, Modern Philology, Criticism, Notes and Queries* (England), *Studies in Burke and His Time, Texas Studies in Literature and Language, Restoration and Eighteenth-Century Theatre Research, Novel,* and *Research Studies.* He has co-authored a textbook, *Functional English* (with G. A. Cevasco and J. P. Franzetti) and has written the Introduction to Robert Dodsley's *Essay on Fable* (with J. K. Welcher) for the Augustan Reprint Society.

Professor Dircks has presented papers and conducted conferences at meetings of scholarly associations here and abroad, including the Modern Language Association of America, the International Association for the Study of Anglo-Irish Literature, the American Society for Eighteenth-Century Studies, the Northeast Modern Language Association, and the Northeast American Society for Eighteenth-Century Studies.

Preface

This study is designed to provide an introduction to Henry Fielding in such a way as to integrate his central ideas and vision of life as they are expresssed in his work as dramatist, journalist, pamphleteer, and novelist. Emphasis has been placed on Fielding's major works, omitting discussion of lesser efforts and *An Essay on Conversation* and *An Essay on the Knowledge of the Characters of Men* in the interest of giving fuller treatment to the novels. Only those biographical details needed to provide a coherent sketch of his career have been included, since two substantial biographies, those of Wilbur Cross and F. Homes Dudden, already provide biographical information that is adequate for all but the specialist in Fielding biography.

The book does not attempt to present a particular thesis about Fielding's work, but it does provide a reading that is, on the one hand, personal and, on the other, informed by the vast amount of scholarship and criticism on Fielding that has appeared in recent years. The debt of any commentator on Fielding to the work of other scholars cannot be adequately defined, and hints and suggestions unknowingly drawn from a great variety of sources can be only generally acknowledged. Similarly, over the years, the staffs of the great research libraries, the New York Public, the Folger, The Huntington in San Marino, the British Library, and those of Columbia, Harvard, Yale, and Princeton, have silently and often unknowingly provided incalculable help.

As a basic primary source of Fielding's work, I have used the sixteen-volume *Complete Works* edited by Ernest Henley because it is the most widely available since its reprinting in 1967. I have in general, however, indicated within the text the sources of quotations by chapter reference and similar methods rather than by page number, so that they might be traced in any reliable edition of Fielding's works. I have also kept notes and references to a minimum. One exception to my use of the Henley edition has been *Shamela,* not included in that edition, for which I have employed that edited by Sheridan Baker.

Richard J. Dircks

St. John's University

Chronology

1707   Henry Fielding born at Sharpham Park, Somerset.

1719   Education at Eton begins, continuing until 1724.

1728   *The Masquerade, a Poem,* Fielding's first published work, under the name of Lemuel Gulliver, Poet Laureate to the King of Lilliput. *Love in Several Masques,* Fielding's first play produced at Drury Lane on February 16. In March registers as a student at the University of Leyden.

1729   Leaves Leyden in the summer and in the fall goes to London.

1730   *The Temple Beau* produced at Goodman's Fields. *The Author's Farce; and The Pleasures of the Town* produced at the Haymarket. *Tom Thumb* produced at the Haymarket. The play was substantially revised and published with a Preface, Prologue, and Epilogue. *Rape upon Rape; or, The Justice Caught in His Own Trap.* The play was later altered and the title changed to *The Coffee-House Politician; or, The Justice Caught in His Own Trap.*

1731   *The Tragedy of Tragedies; or, The Life and Death of Tom Thumb the Great,* a revision of *Tom Thumb,* with annotations by H. Scriblerus Secundus. *The Letter-Writers; or, A New Way to Keep a Wife at Home,* at the Haymarket. *The Welsh Opera; or, The Grey Mare the Better Horse* produced at the Haymarket. *The Genuine Grub Street Opera,* a revised version of *The Welsh Opera* published in August. *The Grub Street Opera,* another version, published later in the year.

1732   *The Lottery* produced at Drury Lane. *The Modern Husband* produced at Drury Lane. *The Old Debauchees* and *The Covent Garden Tragedy* produced at Drury Lane. *The Mock Doctor,* a farce adapted from Molière, produced at Drury Lane.

1733   *The Miser,* an adaptation of Molière, produced at Drury Lane.

1734   *The Intriguing Chamber Maid* produced at Drury Lane. *Don Quixote in England* produced at the Haymarket. Marries Charlotte Cradock on November 28.

1735   *An Old Man Taught Wisdom; or, The Virgin Unmasked* produced at Drury Lane. *The Universal Gallant; or The Different Husbands* produced unsuccessfully at Drury Lane.

1736   *Pasquin. A Dramatic Satire on the Times; Being the Rehearsal of Two Plays, viz. a Comedy call'd The Election, and a Tragedy call'd The Life and Death of Common-Sense* produced at the Haymarket with great success. *Tumble Down Dick: or, Phaeton in the Suds* produced at the Haymarket as an afterpiece to *Pasquin.*

1737   *Eurydice* produced unsuccessfully at Drury Lane. *The Historical Register for the Year 1736* produced at the Haymarket as afterpiece to Lillo's *The Fatal Curiosity* on March 21. *Eurydice Hiss'd* produced as an afterpiece to *The Historical Register.* The Licensing Act passed on June 21. Undertakes the study of law at the Middle Temple in November.

1739   Begins to edit the *Champion* on November 15 and continues until June 1741.

1740   Supervises and contributes to the translation of *The Military History of Charles XII, King of Sweden* in three volumes. Called to the Bar on June 20.

1741   *An Apology for the Life of Mrs. Shamela Andrews* published under the mock name of Conny Keyber.

1742   *The History of the Adventures of Joseph Andrews, and of his Friend Mr. Abraham Adams* published on February 22, with a second edition in August, a third in March 1743.

1743   *The Wedding Day* produced at Drury Lane on February 17. *Miscellanies* in three volumes published on April 12. The volumes contain *Jonathan Wild* and *A Journey from This World to the Next.*

1744   Writes the "Preface" for Sarah Fielding's *David Simple.* Death of Fielding's wife.

1745   Begins to edit *The True Patriot; and the History of Our Own Times* in November and continues until June, 1746. Also writes a number of pamphlets in support of the government against the Jacobites.

1747   Marries Mary Daniel. Begins editing the *Jacobite's Journal* in December and continues until November 1748.

1749   Commissioned magistrate for the County of Middlesex in January. *The History of Tom Jones, a Foundling.* Four editions published by December. *A Charge Delivered to the Grand Jury* . . . *on the 29th of June, 1749* and *A True State of the Case of Bosavern Penlez.*

1751   *An Enquiry into the Causes of the Late Increase of Robbers* published in January. *Amelia,* Fielding's last novel, published in December.

1752   The *Covent Garden Journal* published from January 4 to November 25.

1753   *A Proposal for Making an Effectual Provision for the Poor,* published in January and dedicated to Henry Pelham. *A Clear State of the Case of Elizabeth Canning* published in March. Prepares and executes a plan for reducing crime in London.

1754   Becomes seriously ill and undertakes a voyage to Lisbon for his health, between June 26 and August 7. *The Life of Mr. Jonathan Wild the Great. A New Edition with Considerable Corrections and Additions,* published on March 19. It is a revised version of *Jonathan Wild* published in the *Miscellanies,* softening the satire directed against Walpole in the earlier version. Fielding dies at Junqueira, near Lisbon, on October 8.

1755   *The Journal of a Voyage to Lisbon* published posthumously together with *A Fragment of a Comment on Lord Bolingbroke's Essays.*

Chapter One

The Energy of Youth

Henry Fielding was born on April 22, 1707, into a family that enabled him to flirt with but not truly embrace the high society of England. His great-grandfather, George Fielding, whose youngest son, John, was the grandfather of the novelist, was the Earl of Desmond, but that title and, apparently, the wealth of the family descended through the line of his oldest son, William. Henry's mother, Sarah, was the daughter of Sir Henry Gould, who left his daughter a sufficient amount of money for her and her husband, Edmund Fielding, to purchase an estate in East Stour in North Dorset, where the family moved when Henry was less than three years old.

When Sarah Fielding died in 1718, the children came under the care of their great-aunt, Catherine Cottington, who was the sister of Lady Gould, and a short time later his father went to London, where he was remarried, this time to a Roman Catholic. Upon his return to East Stour, the family separated, and Henry was sent to Eton for his education. Among the lasting acquaintances he made there was George Lyttleton, who rose to high position in English politics and retained a close association with the novelist. Leaving Eton in 1724, Henry lived at Lady Gould's residence in Salisbury but made frequent trips to London. Among his relatives was a cousin, the famous Lady Mary Wortley Montagu, who shared his interest in literature and the theater, and to whom he dedicated his first comedy, *Love in Several Masques*.

Fielding's effort to embark on a literary career began before he left England to undertake his studies in literature at the University of Leyden in Holland. Adopting the name of Lemuel Gulliver as the supposed author, he published his first poem, *The Masquerade*, inscribed to C---t H--d--g-r, John James Heidegger who at that time conducted public masquerades attended largely by the upper classes. Fielding's satiric thrust at this kind of notorious entertainment is supported by his use of the octosyllabic comic verse form of Samuel Butler's *Hudibras*, a meter which

Jonathan Swift had also used with telling effect. In the poem, which takes the shape of the reflections of a man of quality who, in the guise of a poor poet, takes a chair to the masquerade, is an early treatment of a theme that is central to Fielding's thought, the conflict between appearance and reality.

Early Comedies

The inspiration of the Restoration dramatists, William Congreve and William Wycherley, is evident in *Love in Several Masques,* which was well mounted at the Theatre-Royal, Drury Lane, with the famous Anne Oldfield, Robert Wilks, and Colley Cibber acting the principal roles. The comedy was produced immediately after the extremely successful run of John Vanbrugh's *The Provok'd Husband,* which had been performed on twenty-eight successive nights. Fielding's play might have benefited from this fact, for Mrs. Oldfield, who was the chief asset of *The Provok'd Husband,* also starred in *Love in Several Masques,* and her presence might well have drawn audiences into the theater to see Fielding's comedy. Fielding's play ran for four nights, not an entirely shameful display, but hardly an indication of marked success.

His debt to Wycherley and Congreve is suggested in Fielding's "Preface" where, with humility proper to a fledgling dramatist, he notes that the difficulties he faced "seemed rather to require the superior force of a Wycherley, or a Congreve, than of a raw and unexperienced pen." Congreve, the later of the two models, seems to have provided the stronger inspiration, and little ingenuity is required to trace the influence of *Love for Love*[1] on Fielding's comedy. Fielding's play focuses on the artificial world of high life and sets up a series of contrasts. Merital, who takes an idealistic view of love and a sympathetic one of women, contrasts with Malvil, who allows no virtue to women and little merit to love. These male characters are appropriately matched by their opposites, Helena, whose softer nature is appropriate for Merital, and Vermilia, whose cynicism is a fit match for Malvil. In addition, the relative merits of country life and city life in promoting romance are suggested by the characters of Wisemore, the country gentleman whose study of philosophy informs his life and provides him with a theoretical conception of love, and the woman he loves and has followed to town, Lady Matchless, a beautiful widow so soured on life by her former husband that she vows to revenge herself on all men. Appropriate complications develop when Sir Positive Trap destines his ward, Helena, for Sir Apish Simple rather than Merital because the alliance would be financially advantageous. The machinations and greed of

Catchit conspire to convince Malvil that he is rivaled for the affections of Vermilia by Merital. Rattle, reminiscent of Congreve's Tattle in *Love for Love,* competes with Wisemore for the love of Lady Matchless. Finally, Lord Formal contributes the comic dimensions of the inevitable fop. The usual mistakes in identity and eventual recognitions bring the proper parties together.

The play is not substantially original in concept, nor is its structure as inventive and supportive of the intrigues created as are the plots of Congreve. *Love in Several Masques,* however, contains a good story and characterization sufficient to support a successful comedy. Even at the early age of nineteen Fielding had a good sense of dialogue and a wit capable of supporting a substantial satiric assault on the manners of high life. The brilliance and fluidity of Congreve's comic dialogue is missing, but this need not have been a fatal problem. The great weakness of the play is that it imitates a form suitable to another era. Even Congreve's *The Way of the World* [2] was relatively unsuccessful when first produced but picked up popularity as the years passed to become a brilliant representative of an obsolete society. Audiences look to new plays for a picture of their own time, while tolerating anachronistic views in older plays. *Love in Several Masques* reflected nothing of the middle-class society then frequenting the theater, and, in its portrayal of the world of upper society, it was out of date. The product of youthful reading, it was not a vehicle that could successfully project the comic genius of Fielding.

Wisely, Fielding seems to have recognized his fundamental lack of preparedness to continue his work in the literary or theatrical world without formal study, and in the spring of 1728 he left for Leyden, where he read in the faculty of letters until the summer of 1729. The effect of his study of the classics is particularly recognizable in his later work. Returning to London, he developed a valuable association with James Ralph, who taught him much about urban existence. His relatively brief period of formal university study combined with the practical wisdom achieved through firsthand experience in London life to help him undertake another effort at a dramatic career. Probably because it had been rejected at Drury Lane, he produced *The Temple Beau* at Goodman's Fields on January 26, 1730. It was performed thirteen times during that season, a success significant enough to encourage him to continue to write for the theater. For the student of Fielding, the drama contains a number of interesting foreshadowings of the direction his literary career was to take.

The Temple Beau reflects the dramatist's continuing debt to Congreve. A comedy of manners, it followed the trend of the times, for a high percentage of the plays offered at Goodman's Fields that season were successful examples of that type. *The Temple Beau* contains little that is reminiscent of the Restoration and, although it cannot be considered a true comedy of sentiment, it shares with that dramatic genre the shifts in sensibility that are frequently associated with it. Most important, it espouses a highly moralistic, even sentimental view of marriage. Although a cynical picture of love is embodied in the character of Wilding, the temple beau who is abetted in his actions by Lady Gravely and Lady Lucy Pedant, the characters of Veromil and Bellaria support an idealistic view of constancy and love.

The framework of *The Temple Beau* is the fable of Wilding, who has been sent by his father, Sir Harry Wilding, to study law at the Temple, but who has used the opportunity to carry on a life of extravagance and pleasure by falsely billing his father for books and other necessities. When Sir Harry comes to town to see his son, Wilding is compelled to resort to a series of tricks to mask his real activities, all of which succeed for a time, but ultimately fail. Within this frame is the important story of love that centers on attitudes toward that passion expressed by the lives of three former Oxford students, who are friends, or at least acquaintances, of Wilding. Veromil, Valentine, and Young Pedant each represents a different response to love. Veromil, a sentimental idealist, is about to leave for the Continent to marry Bellaria, who, unknown to him, has arrived in London. Valentine, his close friend, is scheduled to be married the next day to the lovely Clarissa but, having caught sight of the more beautiful Bellaria, has had a change of heart. He does not know, of course, of the relationship that has developed between Veromil and Bellaria. Finally, Young Pedant, whose parents would have him marry Bellaria, has steeped himself in learning and finds the idea of marriage so frightening that his only recourse is a return to his books. When Wilding is finally suggested as a mate for Bellaria, all four young men focus on that object. Matters are further complicated romantically by the efforts of Lady Gravely and Lady Lucy Pedant to pursue amours with Wilding, and they reach a climax as Wilding, forced to find quarters that contain books in order to fool his father, borrows the rooms of Young Pedant. Mistaken assignations, marriage plans, and the effort to fool Pedant bring all the principals together in Young Pedant's quarters. A hectic scene, including a brief threat of a duel between Valentine and Veromil, serves to resolve the love complications and to reveal the truth about Wilding to his father. Veromil marries his beloved Bellaria; Clarissa accepts the repentant Valentine; Wilding reveals a good side to his nature by interposing in the fight between Veromil and Valentine when his father is in danger, and Young Pedant returns to the University.

The fifth act borders on the kind of burlesque exuberance that marks the spirit of Fielding's novels, particularly *Joseph Andrews,* and, in introducing the law and its manipulation as a source of comic plot entanglement, the dramatist focuses on an aspect of eighteenth-century life that he subsequently exploits in a much more serious way in his novels. The relationship of fortune to happiness is studied through the actions of those who pursue Bellaria for her money, versus the pure sentimental attachment of Veromil who loves her for herself. The restoration of the fortune that his brother had taken from Veromil through the false testimony of Pincet assures the happiness of the lovers by buttressing their mutual fidelity with financial stability.

The usual characterization of *The Temple Beau* as an immature work has tended to turn the student of Fielding away from a drama that is of considerable importance in tracing his intellectual and artistic development. His ability to read the atmosphere of his own day and to exploit a genre successfully is clearly evident. The sympathy of the play is with the middle-class idealization of marriage that is characteristic of the growing sentiment of the changing theatrical audience. The sentimental scene in which Valentine and Veromil idealize both love and friendship (act 4, scene 10) is much in the spirit of the time. Fielding's robust view of life is evident and suggests the intellectual strength that will inform his comic view of life throughout his subsequent career. Finally, the spirit of burlesque and farcical vision, evident in the wild gyrations of the fifth act, suggests that Fielding is well prepared for the imminent shift to farce that he makes in response to the theatrical necessities of the time. James Ralph's "Prologue" to *The Temple Beau* indicates his awareness of the shift in sensibility toward farce that was occurring in the theater, and that such an awareness was undoubtedly shared by Fielding. If, as Ralph suggests, ". . . only farce, and show, will now go down / and Harlequin's the darling of the town," Fielding is prepared both pragmatically and artistically to shift in that direction.

Success with Farce

When Fielding returned from Leyden he had with him the manuscript of a play, *Don Quixote in England,* but found that the management of Drury Lane regarded it as inadequate for the stage. When *The Temple Beau* had been similarly looked on with disfavor by the same management, he had turned to the new theater at Goodman's Fields, headed by Henry Giffard, but that theater soon ran into difficulties that threatened its successful continuation. Fielding was forced to look elsewhere and this time turned to the Little Theatre in the Haymarket, where a wild farce, *Hurlothrumbo*,[3] had been recently produced with great success. This unique work was a strange phenomenon without recognizable dramatic structure, traditional plot, or usual patterns of characterization, but it combined all these liabilities into an entertaining vehicle that made the audience laugh. In following *Hurlothrumbo* Fielding had to please an audience that found an absurd form of comedy to its taste.

Fielding's response to this set of circumstances was *The Author's Farce; and The Pleasures of the Town,* two distinct comedies, loosely linked by the familiar rehearsal format and satirically aimed at two familiar targets, the shortcomings of the publishing and theatrical world in which he was attempting to make a living, and the inane activities with which eighteenth-century London was then entertaining itself.

The first part of the play concerns the plight of Harry Luckless who is being pressed by his landlady, Mrs. Moneywood, for payment of his rent. Harry is only a shadow of what he was when he arrived three months earlier as a dashing young man in a gold-laced coat, accompanied by a servant. His success has not measured up to his appearance, and, virtually destitute, Harry has only one hope of avoiding financial disaster, a comedy that he plans to stage. He has offered it to Mr. Keyber, but this thinly disguised Colley Cibber, then manager of Drury Lane, has no time to see him. His efforts to publish the play have been similarly rebuffed, for Mr. Bookweight informs him that a play that has not yet been staged has no value. Finally, Marplay and Sparkish, the managers at Covent Garden, allow him to read the play. Marplay, who alters the plays he produces in a ridiculous fashion, represents Cibber, who was notorious for play doctoring, while Sparkish stands for Robert Wilks, Cibber's fellow manager. The play is, in the end, rejected, not because it lacks value, but because the author has no support from political or social circles. Pushed to the wall, Luckless now brings the farce to the Haymarket where it is accepted by the management, and, for this reason, by Bookweight as well. Fielding describes the factory where Bookweight produces his volumes, drawing comic pictures of Dash, Blotpage, Quibble, and Index, all of whom busily labor as hacks under imperious direction.

When the scene shifts to the Haymarket Theatre, the rehearsal of *The Pleasures of the Town* is taking place in the form of a puppet show. The format of the drama is a descent into the underworld to the throne of Nonsense where all of the current pleasures and entertainments of the town appear to seek the favor of the goddess. Signior Opera, Don Tragedio, Sir Farcical, Monsieur Pantomime, Hurlothrumbo, Mrs.

Novel, and Orator Henley, all make their appearances. The farce thus thrusts at a broad range of current entertainments before ending in a wild scene in which reality and nonreality merge. Sir John Bindover and the Constable appear to arrest Luckless for abusing Nonsense, and everything merges into a confused world as Luckless suggests that the Constable become the Chief Justice of Bantam, and Mrs. Moneywood the Queen of Brentford. All ends with a dance.

The combined plays of *The Author's Farce and the Pleasures of the Town* introduce an aspect of Fielding's talent that he had not yet truly exploited, his sense of how the ridiculous and the absurd could create theatrical entertainment. His farcical sense is not without its wisdom, however, and before the realistic satire of the first two acts erupts into seeming absurdity in the third, Fielding introduces a serious view of how the pursuit of wealth and pleasure may be related to the softer emotions of genuine love. Mrs. Moneywood, exasperated at the interest her daughter, Harriot, has in Luckless, explodes:

"No woman of sense was ever in love with any thing but a man's pocket. What, I suppose he has filled your head with a pack of romantic stuff of streams and dreams, and charms and arms. I know this is the stuff they all run on with, and so run into our debts, and run away with our daughters.—Come, confess, are not you two to live in a wilderness together in love? Ah! thou fool! thou wilt find he will pay thee in love, just as he has paid me in money."

Harriot's response is the response of the impractical sentimentalist: "Well, madam, and I would sooner starve with the man I love than ride in a coach and six with him I hate" (act 2, scene 10). In the midst of farce and absurdity Fielding introduces a motif that he will seriously explore in his major fiction, the need to reject the pragmatic lure of wealth for the more enduring warmth of love. While mastering the techniques of farce and demonstrating his ability to make men laugh, Fielding very early in his career gives evidence of a developing moral and social consciousness that not only will condemn the foolish aspects of contemporary life, but will also recognize the consequences of the absurd manifestations of vanity in individual lives.

Capitalizing on the popularity of the play, Fielding rapidly put together a short two-act afterpiece to accompany *The Author's Farce.* His new effort, *Tom Thumb,* ultimately outstripped its predecessor in both quality and popularity. His new vehicle satirizes the heroic dramas popular at the time. Nathaniel Lee's *The Rival Queens,* John Banks's *The Albion Queens,* and James Thomson's *Sophonisba*[4] were currently appearing at either Lincoln's Inn Fields or Drury Lane, and Dryden's heroic dramas were well known to the audience. For this reason, the diminutive Tom Thumb as the hero of a heroic tragedy was a promising subject for farce. The play, a fine parody of heroic theater, is set in the time of King Arthur to whose court the hero, Tom Thumb, returns in triumph. In reward for his heroic action, the king promises him the hand of the princess Huncamunca, but this action arouses the jealous wrath of Queen Dollalolla who has formed a secret love for the hero. Things are further complicated by having Lord Grizzle, who loves the princess, conspire with the queen to prevent the intended marriage. Huncamunca is delighted to learn from her father that he wishes her to marry Tom Thumb, and she thus becomes her mother's rival. Although there is a mistaken report that Tom has been killed, he eventually appears, only to be subsequently swallowed by a cow. When the ghost of Tom Thumb materializes, he is ridiculously slain a second time by Grizzle. One character kills another until the king alone remains to slay himself, thus leaving the stage a mass of carnage. The farce was immediately successful and solidified Fielding's great popularity. Reasons for its success extended beyond the surface aptness of its parody of heroic drama. King Arthur is greatly reduced in stature and is little more than a ruffian. All of the characters utter crude sentiments in heroic language suggesting the real coarseness of much of the sentiment to be found in the heroic plays. In the end, it is Fielding's sense of fun and his ability to inject high good humor into the events that give the play its real life. Fielding instinctively recognized the potential of *Tom Thumb* to be more than a brief afterpiece and he immediately set about its revision. He added scenes, altered the catastrophe by eliminating Tom Thumb's ghost and introducing the ghost of Gaffer Thumb, and enlarged the farce to three acts.

When *Tom Thumb* was published, it was accompanied by a Prologue, an Epilogue, and a Preface. An altered version of the play was produced on March 24, 1731, as *The Tragedy of Tragedies; or, The Life and Death of Tom Thumb the Great*. This new version, published as the second edition of the play, contains a new Preface by H. Scriblerus Secundus that provides a set of mock-critical annotations by that supposed author. From a literary point of view, the final published version is of great importance as it is Fielding's entrance into the mock-heroic convention so effectively exploited by Swift, Pope, and the other Scriblerians. *The Tragedy of Tragedies*, in addition to being a masterpiece of satire, became an excellent stage vehicle, as its great success on the eighteenth-century stage demonstrated.

Fielding's sense of the ludicrous and his penetrating insights into contemporary life are combined in consistently fresh and original ways. The fertility of his creative instincts had by this time become abundantly clear and gave promise of a great artistic career. Capitalizing on his popularity, he brought out, at the Haymarket, production after production. His next comedy is somewhat reminiscent of the style of *The Temple Beau* in its interest in the practitioners of the law, but is more narrowly focused on the common and often scandalous institution of Justice of the Peace. Its original title, *Rape upon Rape; The Justice Caught in his Own Trap*, was altered when its emphasis on rape met with objections, and it finally emerged as *The Coffee-House Politician; or, The Justice Caught in his Own Trap*. The satire moves in two directions, one through the character of the corrupt Justice Squeezum, and the second through Mr. Politic, the type of individual who neglects his responsibilities to spend most of his time at the coffeehouse discussing the intricacies of recent news. The lives of the two men intersect when Hilaret, the daughter of Politic, is brought before Squeezum as a result of the constable's interruption of Ramble's attempt to seduce her. The main thrust of the satire moves against the criminal justice system, attacking both the way prisoners are brought into custody, often without their having committed any crime, and the disreputable justices they face.

A secondary object of Fielding's attack is the insanity of Politic's preoccupation with news. He has neglected his duties because of an exaggerated interest in events that have no real importance in his life. The future of his daughter is forgotten while he pursues his hobby of learning about the latest happenings in distant parts of the world. Only the impending tragedy of her arrest brings him to his senses. In the character of Ramble we also find an essentially good person, but one who acts before he thinks and thus becomes embroiled in problems he might have avoided by prudent reflection. Fielding's satire in *The Coffee-House Politician*, for this reason, concerns not only the external forces of corruption that influence the lives of the citizenry at large, but also those internal forces that serve to undermine the lives of individual people. Politic and Ramble are as dangerous to themselves and to those close to them because of their neglect of duty or failure to think before acting, as is the constable or justice who acts out of deliberate malice.

The Coffee-House Politician was a return to comedy from the preoccupation with farce that had begun to dominate Fielding's career. During the 1731–32 theatrical season the enlarged version of *Tom Thumb, The Tragedy of Tragedies*, was produced. New additions to the play proved popular, particularly the addition to the dramatis personae of Glumdalca, her rivaling the queen and the princess for the affections of the diminutive hero, and the parody of the Octavia-Cleopatra scene in John Dryden's *All for Love*.[5] Although Tom's ghost is eliminated from the ending of the drama, a new ghost, that of Tom's father, Gaffer Thumb, is added to warn the king that Lord Grizzle, motivated by jealousy, is raising forces against him. Curiously enough, the old ending in which Tom's ghost is slain was retained in performances of the farce at Goodman's Fields, and both versions were simultaneously performed at different theaters during the season. Whether or not, in the demise of Tom Thumb, a parallel with the contemporary "Great Man," Robert Walpole, could be recognized, is a matter of conjecture. Although critics have called attention to this possibility, its recognition as such during the years of its early history is problematical, and no such notice of it seems to have been taken by the ministry. A brief farce by Fielding called *The Letter-Writers; or, A New Way to Keep a Wife at Home* was presented as an afterpiece to *The Tragedy of Tragedies* but failed and was quickly withdrawn.

Political Farce

It was impossible or, at the very least, extremely unlikely that Fielding could avoid being involved in political satire. Those subjects that he attacked—the heroic play, the assorted entertainments of the town, the criminal justice system—all of them major aspects of contemporary life—had already been dealt with vigorously. The world of politics was an obvious object for Fielding's satiric pen. Robert Walpole, because of his position as prime minister, had ultimately to be the target. To feel that there was any personal animus between Walpole and Fielding would be unrealistic. Quite the contrary seems to have been true, and the dramatist did, in fact, dedicate *The Modern Husband* to him.

Walpole, however, typified much that was wrong with politics in general, not necessarily because one politician was more corrupt than another, but because the system gave ample opportunity for the corrupt tendencies of human nature to surface. Robert Walpole had come to power in 1721 and, from that time on, had been in effect the prime minister, although that title had not yet entered into common usage. He was a good complement to King George II and his wife Queen Caroline, for they had little interest in the day-to-day workings of government and were content to leave such matters to the firm hand of the minister. Walpole had many talents that suited him for government, not the least of which was a logical mind and a great capacity for hard work. He was a consummate financial expert and, largely because of his ability to know and understand people, was an effective leader of Parliament. He also cared little for religion or matters of the spirit. Not a man of subtle social views, he saw government as a means of keeping the nation running on an even keel. He was the supreme pragmatist in government and an adroit advocate of materialism. Apparently personally honest, whatever questionable practices he might have engaged in to remain in power or to govern effectively, he did not seek to enrich himself at the public till, but was more interested in power than in money. He carried on an open and notorious affair with his mistress, Molly Skerrett, a circumstance that had little effect on his political fortunes.

Walpole was not the sort of man Fielding could admire, and even a casual acquaintance with the novelist's work provides unmistakable evidence that the sense of values of the two men were diametrically opposed. Fielding, a dedicated Christian although not a lover of religious form and ritual, had a profound sense of the spirit, and saw in the heart and the natural instincts of the individual much of the basis for action. His view of love and of the individual left little room for tolerating the open relationship that Walpole had with his mistress. Fielding, moreover, hated sham and pretense, both of which were public marks of the successful politician. In hitting at the political system, therefore, Fielding could not avoid offending the most accomplished practitioner in that system, and he joined the crescendo of criticism that was rising against the ministry.

Fielding's first direct and major political satire was *The Welsh Opera: or The Grey Mare the Better Horse,* which was performed with *Tom Thumb* at the Haymarket on April 22, 1731. The prose dialogue of the play is interspersed with songs, a format popularly established by *The Beggar's Opera.* Setting the scene in Wales justifies the use of a heavy accent resembling that of George II. The plot is a simple one concerning the fight which two servants of Squire Ap-Shinken and his henpecking wife have over Robin's mistress, Sweetissa. Mrs. Ap-Shinken provides satiric moments, for she continually occupies herself with talking to Parson Puzzletext about religion. Her son, Owen, is a mischievous individual who stirs up matters by writing a letter purporting to be from William, the groom, to Sweetissa sparking a jealous reaction by Robin and involving both servants in a battle in which they fight and kick each other without causing much discernible harm.

The whole is a superficial political allegory. The Ap-Shinken household is the English nation presided over by the king and queen respectively.

Both are favorably drawn, but the squire's lack of concern for his household suggests the amiable lack of concern of George II for the details of government. Robin, the dishonest butler, to whom the running of the house is left, is clearly Robert Walpole, and William, the groom with whom he quarrels, is Pulteney the opposition leader. The battle the two engage in over Sweetissa is clearly suggestive of political warfare, and Sweetissa has been thought to resemble Molly Skerrett, Walpole's mistress. The play may be seen as a general attack on the dishonesty inherent in politics, for Pulteney, the opposition leader, is no more honest than Walpole as they are allegorically portrayed. On the other hand, the blanket suggestion that national politics and leading politicians were both foolish and dishonest was clearly more harmful to the party in power than to that of the opposition.

Perhaps of even greater importance than the details of the play itself was the drama with which it was eventually coupled when presented to the public, *The Fall of Mortimer*.[6] Roger de Mortimer, the first Earl of March, was notorious in English history for having conspired to keep King Edward II under subjection in his youth before he was old enough to take over control of the country. With the Queen Mother, Mortimer had been the virtual ruler of the nation before being hanged. To the opposition, his corrupt practices suggested a parallel with those of Walpole. The fragment of a play on Mortimer by Ben Jonson had been completed and brought up to date by an unknown playwright, often thought to be the minor dramatist William Hatchett, and had been fashioned in such a way as to suggest the inherent parallel between Mortimer and Walpole. The presentation of *The Welsh Opera* as an afterpiece to *The Fall of Mortimer* thus amounted to a strong attack on Walpole and his administration. The ministry moved against the play when it was expanded to a three-act drama and renamed *The Grub-Street Opera*. Not only was that play kept from the stage, but the government moved vigorously to prevent further performances of other plays at the Haymarket. For all intents and purposes, that theater could no longer function as an outlet for Fielding's dramas, and he moved to Drury Lane for an extremely active 1731–32 season.

Social Farce and Traditional Comedy

Convinced that if he was to continue in the theater, he had to abandon political farce and satire, at least temporarily, Fielding turned to social farce and traditional comedy. In establishing himself as the leading playwright of the day, he had achieved most of his success without recourse to politics and, having apparently patched up his relationship with Cibber, looked forward to a promising season.

Fielding's first new play at Drury Lane was *The Lottery,* a gay ballad opera satirizing the penchant for gambling that found an outlet in the state lotteries. It deals with the fate of a country girl who is convinced that her ticket will win. Appearing as a wealthy daughter of fortune, she is tricked into a fake marriage by Lord Lace, but when it is discovered that she has no fortune and he no title, the slight comedy ends with her marrying a loyal country lover. The play was immediately successful, Fielding demonstrating that in social satire he could find the ingredients of success.

From a literary point of view, Fielding's next play was far more ambitious, for in it he no longer toyed with light farces and brief afterpieces, but concerned himself with a serious five-act drama. *The Modern Husband,* presented at Drury Lane on February 14, 1732, was in some ways a daring experiment for Fielding, since it was not a comedy of humors or of manners, but a drama of sentiment, focusing realistically on the shortcomings of society's treatment of marriage and love. The high life of Mr. and Mrs. Modern is partly supported by her cheating at cards, but that income is not enough to continue the standard of living they desire. In order to maintain their way of life Modern sells his wife to Lord Richly for fifteen hundred pounds, but when that sum is exhausted he plans to extort money from the lord by having him discovered in a compromising situation. This scheme fails, for Richly has grown tired of Mrs. Modern and can therefore not be tricked. In the midst of their conversation, however, Richly offers to pay Mrs. Modern handsomely if she will deliver Mrs. Bellamant so that he might seduce her. A virtuous woman, she is married to a weak though basically decent husband who has formed an extramarital alliance with Mrs. Modern.

Modern hits upon these circumstances to suggest that they use the same device on Bellamant that they had planned for Richly. When Mrs. Modern finds this solution unpalatable, her husband persuades his footman to swear that he has found Bellamant and Mrs. Modern together. The drama ends with the discovery of this attempted fraud, the reconciliation of the Bellamants, and the exoneration of Mrs. Modern because she has been corrupted by her husband. A minor plot, dealing with sentimental love, finds Lord Richly's daughter, Lady Charlotte Gaywit, married to Captain Bellamant, and his son Gaywit to the Bellamant's daughter.

The Modern Husband deals with a distasteful subject in a serious and realistic fashion. Part of the genre of middle-class comedy, it aims not at laughter but sentimental instruction. There is little in the story to amuse an audience, and most of the play presents a serious moral evaluation of a vice that may have been common in Fielding's day. The play ran for fifteen nights, a relatively short run for Fielding's plays at this time, but quite a respectable showing for serious drama.

After *The Modern Husband,* Fielding composed three shorter works for the summer season at Drury Lane. *The Old Debauchees* and *The Covent-Garden Tragedy* appeared together. The first was a sordid play dealing with a story similar to one notorious at the time in which a French Jesuit priest, Father Girard, had seduced Catherine Cadière through the use of sorcery. Using only the skeleton of this incident, Fielding fashions the tale of a Jesuit whose attempt to seduce a young girl is prevented when the girl's lover substitutes himself for her in her bed. The second piece, *The Covent-Garden Tragedy,* burlesques the tragedy, *The Distrest Mother,* which Ambrose Philips had adapted from Racine's *Andromache.* The scenes of the tragedy are coarsely adapted to a brothel to produce a clever and ingenious farce, but one that is not representative of Fielding's best work. *The Covent-Garden Tragedy* was immediately damned by the Drury Lane audience and was replaced by a successful adaptation of Moliere's *Le Médicin malgré lui, The Mock Doctor, or The Dumb lady Cured.* In this version of Molière, Fielding took advantage of popular taste to reduce the French three-act farce to a one-act ballad opera.

In February of the following season Fielding again produced a translation of Molière, this time a full-length adaptation of *The Miser,* with the addition of new scenes. An immediate success, it ran for twenty-six consecutive nights. The play was accompanied by an afterpiece by Fielding. "Deborah, or A Wife for You All," which unfortunately was not published.

Fielding revived his old comedy, *The Author's Farce,* in response to changes in the management of Drury Lane. Barton Booth, who shared the management of the theater with Colley Cibber and Robert Wilks, sold half of his interest to John Highmore, leaving half in his own name. When Wilks died, his widow retained her share, using as her agent John Ellys. Cibber accepted a good offer for his interest from Highmore, passing over his son, Theophilus Cibber, who was acting in the company and fully expected to inherit it from his father. The death of Booth enabled his widow to sell her interest to Henry Giffard as an investment. These changes placed management of the house solidly in the hands of Highmore and explain Fielding's actions in attempting to bolster the sagging fortunes of the theater. In reviving *The Author's Farce,* he updated it to take advantage of the change in management. Wilks, who had been the prototype for Sparkish, is eliminated, and Marplay Junior, representing

Theophilus Cibber, substituted for him. As an afterpiece Fielding added a successful and very popular farce, *The Intriguing Chamber Maid.*

During the following year both Highmore and Mrs. Wilks sold their shares in Drury Lane to Charles Fleetwood, who took over active management. Fielding had prepared *Don Quixote in England,* newly reworked into a ballad opera, for the Drury Lane company, but when the work was set aside and a pantomime extravaganza substituted for it, he offered the piece to the Haymarket theater and it was produced there along with *The Covent-Garden Tragedy.* The new ballad opera in which Don Quixote becomes a candidate for Parliament and which deals with bribery in parliamentary elections, involved Fielding once more in political farce. Although he did not form an alliance with the opposition at this time, Fielding committed himself to move in that direction by dedicating the play to Lord Chesterfield. During the same year, 1734, he married Charlotte Cradock, who brought him much happiness.

Once again, Fielding made the required accommodations at Drury Lane and, on January 17, 1735, produced a new ballad opera, *An Old Man Taught Wisdom; or, The Virgin Unmasked.* The simple story concerns the attempt of a country squire to pass his fortune wisely to his heirs by having his daughter marry the most suitable of his poor relations. He parades before her an apothecary, a dancing master, a singing master, a lawyer, and a student, only to have her exercise her independence by rejecting all of them in favor of a footman whom she has loved for a long time.

The next month Fielding again attempted a long conventional comedy, *The Universal Gallant; or The Different Husbands.* This long drama failed and, after the third night, was withdrawn. Although Fielding was greatly disturbed by the failure of what was a major effort, other concerns intervened and the death of his wife's mother forced him to leave London and embark on what amounted to an extended vacation.

Political Satire

When Fielding returned he offered a new play to Rich at Covent Garden only to have it rejected. Whether or not he offered it to Fleetwood at Drury Lane is uncertain. If the play offered Rich was *Pasquin,* the next comedy Fielding produced, the reason for its rejection is understandable, for in the political climate of the time a play with the political force of *Pasquin* ran considerable risk of opposition from the ministry. Fielding took a bold approach to the problem and, gathering together the players who were performing intermittently at the Haymarket, formed a new company

under the name of "The Great Mogul's Company of English Comedians."
At his own theater, and with his own company, Fielding produced the
comedy that was, on the one hand, to be one of his best and most successful
productions but, on the other, the first of those plays that were destined to
bring the full force of the Walpole administration against him, resulting
in the passage of the Licensing Act and effectively bringing an end to his
career in the theater.

This first production of Fielding's new company at the Haymarket was a
brilliant political satire. He borrowed for himself and his drama the name
Pasquin from the well-known story of the two statues that had once been
erected in Rome, one to Pasquin and the other to Marforio. To the statue of
Pasquin, citizens pinned public complaints; on that of Marforio, they
received their answers. By an extension of this legend, Fielding, the
accuser of society in the guise of Pasquin, produced in 1736 *Pasquin, A
Dramatick Satire on the Times: Being the Rehearsal of Two Plays, viz. A Comedy
Call'd The Election; and a Tragedy Call'd, The Life and Death of Common Sense.*
Fielding again capitalized on the familiar rehearsal format that he had so
successfully used in the past and, by presenting two plays, gave himself an
opportunity to comment on society from two points of view.

At the playhouse, Trapwit and Fustian, authors of the comedy and
tragedy respectively, examine the performances and comment on them in
the company of the critic, Sneerwell. Enlarging on the political theme that
he had introduced in *Don Quixote in England,* Fielding, in the mock-
comedy portion of *Pasquin* entitled "The Election," treats of the corrupt
practices surrounding local elections. The mayor and alderman of a
provincial town discuss the impending election and indicate that they
favor Sir Harry Fox-Chace and Squire Tankard, both of whom are candidates of the Country Party. They are joined by the two candidates of the
Court Party, Lord Place and Colonel Promise, who seek to influence them.
The satire focuses on the two methods of bribery which Fielding portrays
as the order of the day, the direct bribe of passing out money, and the
indirect bribe of enriching the electorate by the ancient practice of
boondoggling. The Court Party wins over the local party by means of the
direct bribe, here symbolized by the squeeze of the hand. Lest the audience
miss the point, Trapwit demands more open bribery: "You, Mr. that act
my Lord, bribe a little more openly, if you please, or the audience will lose
that joke, and it is one of the strongest in my whole play." Having thus
demonstrated the most obvious form of bribery, he informs Fustian that he
must now show the other kind: "You must know, sir, I distinguish bribery
into two kinds; the direct and the indirect: the first you have seen already;

and now, sir, I shall give you a small specimen of the other."[7] He then calls in Sir Harry and the Squire, who promise to build a new house, and thus to enrich the local businessmen by making use of their goods and services. Although the mayor votes for the Court candidates, the election goes to Sir Harry and the Squire. Knowing that he has picked the wrong horse, the mayor still defends his supporting "liberty and property," although he had done so mainly to accede to the demands of both his daughter and his wife. Faced with the disaster of his voting the wrong way, Mrs. Mayoress advises her husband to report out the losers as the winners, consoling her daughter that all will be well: "Dry up your tears, my dear, all will be well; your father shall return my lord and the colonel: and we shall have a controverted election, and we will go to London, my dear."[8] Thus, the local politicians and their families will enjoy a trip to London to settle the matter at the expense of the candidates. The play ends on a capricious note, with Miss Mayoress reporting her marriage to Colonel Promise, to the satisfaction of her mother and father.

Fustian moves quickly on stage with his tragedy, beginning with a "Prologue" that announces that Common Sense will appear on stage. The third act ends with Common Sense reportedly quarreling with Fustian in the Green Room. The play hits strongly at the professions of law and medicine, but its main action concerns Common Sense, as it moves to a confrontation between Queen Common Sense and Queen Ignorance that ends with the slaying of Common Sense, as her followers desert her. Just as the forces of Ignorance seem to triumph, the Ghost of Common Sense appears and is able to drive the followers of Ignorance and Ignorance herself into rapid retreat. The obvious allegory of the play suggests the vast power of even the shadow of Common Sense in a world committed to the forces of Ignorance. Fustian and Sneerwell exchange a brief comment as the play ends, with Sneerwell relieved that Common Sense emerges in the end, in order that the tragedy possess a proper moral, while Fustian realistically observes: "Faith, sir, this is almost the only play where she has got the better lately."

Pasquin was not only a theatrical success but has serious overtones that give it a claim to a higher level of recognition than the usual topical farce. The play is replete with wit and good humor, much of it highly topical in nature and therefore lost on audiences of subsequent centuries. Missing the topical allusions does not, however, seriously minimize the major points Fielding makes both about politics and about human attitudes in general. The satire is not narrowly political, and it suggests that all societies that have an electoral system of government will have greedy and selfish

individuals who will exploit it. The juxtaposition of the battle between
Common Sense and Ignorance with the satire on the election process is no
accident and provides a commentary on the foolishness of the electorate in
misusing a system of government that could bring them much good. For
narrowly selfish reasons, the ignorance of the individual conspires to
destroy the benefits that good government could convey, if common sense
were allowed to prevail in a form that is more than a ghostly shadow.

Pasquin provides fresh evidence of Fielding's mastery of meaningful
farce. It is, moreover, not just politics and society that are attacked; the
dramatic taste of the time is also pilloried, for Tragedy and Comedy, like
Common Sense, are slain in the drama, and emerge again merely as ghosts.
This is, perhaps, more significant than the accompanying attacks on
pantomime, the thrusts made at the staging of plays in general, and hits at
the critics who lay claim to judge them. If taste had declined, as Fielding
suggests, he had learned to accommodate himself to it in brilliant fashion.

Later in the year Fielding added an afterpiece to *Pasquin, Tumble-Down
Dick: or, Phaeton in the Suds.* Characteristically, the farce capitalizes on the
contemporary and is a parody of a pantomime then being presented at
Drury Lane, *The Fall of Phaeton.* It followed one of the current devices of
such entertainments in having serious scenes in which the Greek gods
appear alternate with scenes containing the tricks of Harlequin. Part of
Fielding's technique is to reduce the dignity of the gods by having them
act with the foibles and shortcomings of human beings. Two additional
events of importance occurred for Fielding at the Haymarket this season.
One was a favorable occurrence, his backing the production of George
Lillo's *The Fatal Curiosity,* the other his own unsuccessful production of an
afterpiece at Drury Lane called *"Euridice; or, The Devil Henpecked,"* which
was roundly and immediately damned, and later published in the *Miscellanies* of 1743 as *Eurydice, a Farce; As It Was Damned at the Theatre-Royal in
Drury Lane.*

In his next play Fielding hit upon a clever parody of a current periodical
that reviewed the events of the previous year in a volume that was called
*The Historical Register, Containing an Impartial Relation of All Transactions,
Foreign and Domestic.* This serious summary of the news of the past year
provided a fine basis for a satiric thrust against political and social events of
a current or near-current nature. In the form of a farce of three acts that is
being rehearsed, Fielding uses this familiar format to suggest that, unlike
the published *Historical Register,* his farce will reveal the hidden truth
about political and social events. It was produced at the Haymarket in
March, 1737, as *The Historical Register for the Year 1736.*

The play, like the real *Historical Register,* is made up of events that have no real connection with each other. These scenes are presented at the rehearsal at which the author Medley interprets what is transpiring for the critic, Sourwit, and the foolish patron of the theater, Lord Dapper. The first two scenes are devoted to recent scandalous happenings in the theater, the quarrel between Kitty Clive and Mrs. Theophilus Cibber over who would play the role of Polly in *The Beggar's Opera,* and Cibber's attempt to alter Shakespeare's *King John* into an attack on the Catholic Church in *Papal Tyranny in the Reign of King John.* Fielding then turns to social satire, attacking the current craze of women for the Italian opera singer, Farinelli, and, using a comic portrayal of contemporary auctions, satirizes a wide range of targets. The most important scenes, however, are the two political ones in which he vigorously attacks Walpole and his administration, actually portraying the prime minister on stage and thrusting vigorously at those members of the political opposition who have been bribed to join Walpole's forces. The result is a brilliant and successful satire that goes a step further than *Pasquin* in its political attack.

Fielding did not stop with the *Historical Register* but produced with it an afterpiece that was equally damaging to the administration. Taking advantage of the failure of his own play, *Euridice, or the Devil Henpecked,* during the previous season at Drury Lane, he produced *Eurydice Hiss'd; or, A Word to the Wise.* While on the surface this seemed to be a clever mocking of his own misfortune, he exploited the incident to draw a parallel between the damnation of his farce and the future demise of Walpole. The afterpiece records the adventures of the rise and fall of Mr. Pillage, who is described as a truly great man. The attack on the ignorance of Walpole's administration is made through the slight cover of portraying the politics of Corsica, where new taxes can be levied only among the ignorant, since that characteristic is found among most men. The actions of the politicians are directed by a silent man seated in the corner, obviously the prime minister. The second scene, in which it is suggested that the money raised by politicians is used to corrupt the opposition, is a powerful and telling attack.

An additional occurrence made inevitable the move by the ministry against the theater. The background is important. The opposition newspaper, *Common Sense,* recently founded by Lord Chesterfield, had published a satiric paper, "The Vision of the Golden Rump," in which an idol with a huge rump of gold was adored by the people under a leader whose actions suggested Walpole. Of itself, this would have been insignificant, but when an anonymous play, a two-act farce with a similar title, "The

Golden Rump," was offered to Henry Giffard at Lincoln's Inn Fields, the manager brought it to Walpole, who used it as a pretext for moving toward controlling political satire through the licensing of the stage. Bills working in that direction had previously been introduced in Parliament, but without success. The event of "The Golden Rump" was the catalyst needed to bring about passage of the legislation on June 21, 1737. Political satire and attacks on the ministry were for all practical purposes thus brought to an end.

It is tempting to indulge in the speculation that the Licensing Act brought the career of Fielding the dramatist to an ignominious halt. Undoubtedly, had there been no opposition to his activities, Fielding might well have continued to produce additional dramas like *Pasquin* and *The Historical Register.* It is, however, doubtful that he could have made a permanent career of political satire, or that he could have satisfied his creative instincts in the theater. *The Modern Husband* seems clear evidence that Fielding had aspirations to produce plays other than farces, and that the drama was not an entirely congenial format for his serious commentary on life. The emergence of prose fiction with the development of the novel by Samuel Richardson provided for Fielding an avenue of response that the theater would probably never have offered him. Fielding was one of the great practicing theatrical talents of his time, and his sense of farce and his ability to exploit contemporary happenings was of an order that can well be characterized as genius. Except for *Tom Thumb,* however, succeeding generations have included few of his dramatic productions among his great work or among the artistic masterpieces of England. Even *The Tragedy of Tragedies,* brilliant as it is, is the work of a talent that is only a shadow of that which Fielding was subsequently to display in prose fiction.

Chapter Two

The Maturation of Ideas

Fielding and the Periodical

Fielding became seriously involved in periodical writing in November, 1739, only two years after he had been forced to curtail his work in the theater and had been admitted to the bar at the Middle Temple. The political currents surrounding the ministry and the opposition were ripe for exploitation by Fielding who, at the behest of a syndicate of booksellers, accepted the editorship of a new opposition periodical with James Ralph as assistant editor. Curiously, Fielding left most of the most aggressive political attacks to his collaborator and chose, instead, to express his own views on a wide range of social, religious, ethical, and critical questions. He remained with the *Champion,* as the new periodical was called, for two years, after which he transferred his shares to Ralph, who became its editor.

Following eighteenth-century custom, the main essays of the periodical appeared under an editorial mask, in this case that of Hercules Vinegar, with additional essays and letters from fictitious correspondents and contributors. The formats employed ranged from direct statements to allegorical visions and imaginary voyages, and the tone from serious instruction to humorous comment and satire.

Fielding's other major periodical, the *Covent Garden Journal,* was published from January 4 to November 25, 1752. Between the appearances of these two journals, Fielding expressed his views on society in his *Miscellanies* (1743), his novels, and in social pamphlets such as his *Charge Delivered to the Grand Jury* (1749) and *An Inquiry into the Causes of the Late Increase of Robbers* (1751).

Fielding chose as the fictitious editor of the *Covent Garden Journal* Sir Alexander Drawcansir, Knight, Censor of Great Britain, a name inspired by the hero of George Villiers's Restoration comedy, *The Rehearsal.*[1] The exaggerated personality of Drawcansir, based on the burlesque prototype of John Dryden's hero, Almanzor, from *The Conquest of Granada*,[2] provided Fielding with a useful persona through which to make his satiric thrusts. Fielding's return to the periodical format was at least partly motivated by his desires both to answer literary and political attacks leveled at him, and to find an organ for advertising the Universal Register Office, a business venture in which he was engaged with his blind brother, John.

In addition to the *Champion* and the *Covent Garden Journal*, Fielding was the main contributor to two journals that were highly political in nature. The first, the *True Patriot*, published between November 5, 1745, and June 17, 1746, was formed to counter the unsuccessful rebellion of 1745 in which Prince Charles attempted to restore the monarchy to the Stuart dynasty. The defense of the British constitution and the Protestant religion was Fielding's main reason for the journal, and after the defeat of Charles its usefulness came to an end. A second periodical, the *Jacobite's Journal*, issued between December 5, 1747, and November 5, 1748, was also written in defense of the government. Through its fictitious editor, John Trottplaid, Esq., Fielding ironically attacked the Jacobites by seeming to support them.

Appearance Versus Reality

The proclivity of humanity to place paramount stress on appearance, often at the expense of reality, is a subject prominently explored by Fielding in his periodical essays. He approaches this through an examination of the power of language to deceive as well as to convey precise and accurate meaning. The relationship between language and action is stressed in three numbers of the *Champion,* those of January 12, 15, and 17, 1739–40. In the first he analyzes the word "turn-coat." which originally suggested prudence and frugality in the use of clothing, but which, as applied to the politics of the time, suggests the readiness of public figures to turn their principles inside out as the political climate changes. In the paper of January 15, Fielding reflects on the change that has occurred in the meaning of the word *authority,* from its original Latin sense of awe and respect for the power that personal virtue could inspire in others, to its current sense of power inherent in political office, where personal virtue is often lacking.

In the last of the three papers Fielding discusses the frequent misuse of language to deliberately distort life in such a way that appearance and reality become so confused that an individual often appears to be the opposite of what he is. A similar discussion occurs in the *Covent Garden Journal* of January 14, 1752, in which the author points to common evils that result from the misuse of words, especially in works of morality. The frequent gap that exists between the intended meaning of language and the way in which it is understood leads Fielding to note that traditional words that occur in the works of important preachers such as Barrow, Tillotson, and Clark, for example, "heaven, hell, judgment, righteousness, sin, &c.," are no longer understood in the way these writers intended if the conduct of the average Englishman is considered a yardstick of his beliefs. Fielding is not denying that the words convey a clear literal meaning, but rather, that the common behavior of men indicates that they do not grasp the deeper realities that the words signify; and he thus suggests that men possess a broadly erroneous set of values and use language to mask their true characters under a respectable facade of deceit.

Fielding's sense of the distortion of appearance and reality is more than a matter of language. In the *Champion* of December 11, 1739, he uses a fictitious letter from an anonymous correspondent to Captain Hercules Vinegar to expose the nature of the hypocrite, who is in reality a skeptic, but a constant "frequenter of the church"; and who is delighted at the misfortune of others, but passes for a good-natured person because he expresses "a little verbal pity." The irony is that the hypocrite, who pretends friendship where enmity truly exists, fails to realize that true happiness would result from the real practice of the virtue that he only pretends to embrace.

Fielding considers appearance and reality further in his paper on reputation in the *Champion* of March 4, 1739–40, observing that "though virtue and wisdom be in reality the opposites to folly and vice, they are not so in appearance." The vicious and criminal, largely because they take pains to present an opposite front to the world, are more frequently advanced in society, not for what they are, but for what they appear to be. Since, however, their reputations have been falsely acquired, they cannot bring true happiness, a state achieved only when appearance and reality coincide. The same theme is treated in the *Champion* of April 22, 1740, in which Rich's pantomimes; where surface appearances conceal the machines working behind the puppets, are recognized as symbols of deception in the real world.

When the "Man in the Moon" is presented in the *Champion* of May 10, he distinguishes between the way the world appears in the light of the sun and under the hiding darkness of the night. He alone "can see human nature stript of all its disguises" and observe "the ragged miser and the cheating bankrupt tell their gold, and the fine-drest gentleman alight from his gilt chariot, and go supperless to bed, by the light, or rather darkness of a farthing candle." The "Man in the Moon"'s vision, moreover, perceives that not all is deception, and he offers a contrasting picture of Joan and Hercules Vinegar, who are content with their humble life and who achieve happiness by not seeking to be what they are not.

An important aspect of the distortion of reality is the erroneous picture man has of virtue. The *Champion* for January 24, 1739–40, points to Plato's observation that if men could see virtue naked they would be in love with her. Unfortunately, virtue is often misrepresented, both by those who deny its value and by religious zealots who portray it in a forbidding and unattractive manner. For Fielding, if vice and virtue can be seen as they really are, they are clearly distinguishable, but unfortunately vice, which is often marked by the distortion of truth, "cheats us with the appearance of good." It is only virtue that brings appearances into harmony with reality.

Fielding and Christianity

Fielding looks beyond the temporal value of right conduct, to see it in terms of a future life, thus allying himself with the argument that the Christian divines of his day had advanced against the intrusion of deism and the growing intellectual acceptance of atheism. While the Enlightenment was relying more and more on a view of man expressed by the Roman stoic and, in the process, was generating a distrust of Christianity, Fielding uses Christianity as the basis for affirming the best of ancient wisdom and carries it forward to provide a hope that mankind might achieve happiness both in this world and in the next. Rejecting, on the one hand, the liberal morality of the freethinker and, on the other, the rigidity of Calvinistic Protestantism, Fielding attempts to evolve a reasoned defense of basic Christianity that is both robust and nonecclesiastical. His convictions regarding the existence of God, the certainty of a future life, a belief in an idealistic and dedicated clergy, and, finally, his strong attacks on deists and atheists undergird his basic attitudes toward life, and from these beliefs flow his social and political views. What might be characterized as a sentimentalism that accepts the optimism of Anthony Ashley Cooper, the third Earl of Shaftesbury, and rejects the pessimism of Thomas Hobbes, while it recognizes the values of much of John Locke's political and social philosophy, seems more clearly rooted in orthodox Christianity than in philosophical speculation. Fielding follows Swift in avoiding the lure of the enlightened thinking of the deists, but a clear description of his religious viewpoint is difficult for he constantly avoids both discussing specific religious beliefs and engaging in direct moralizing, relying instead on the indirection of rhetorical structure.

Fielding's conviction that man is destined for a future life runs counter to the reasoned and mechanistic approaches to the study of man that characterized the Enlightenment. By the same token he pays little tribute to the ecclesiastical structure of the Church of England and expresses little or no enthusiasm for regimented worship. In the *Champion* of January 22, 1739–40, Fielding rejects the views of those who looked on religion more from a philosophical than a theological base, and who sought to reduce to rational principles what traditional Christianity saw as God's revelation. He condemns those "philosophers who have, it seems, in direct opposition to that ancient tenet of the Stoic school, that virtue is the greatest good, found out that virtue is the greatest evil . . ." He is greatly influenced by both Locke and Shaftesbury in developing his rational view of political and social problems and in seeking solutions to them. Almost paradoxically, moreover, Locke and Shaftesbury helped to shape the emerging sentimentalism in his assessment of how man should conduct his affairs. The influence they exerted was supplemented by that of some of the articulate clergy of the day, most notably Dr. Robert South and Dr. Isaac Barrow, particularly in shaping his ethical attitudes toward the poor.

The philosophers Fielding condemns have carried on their assault against virtue in two stages: "They have first," he tells us, "endeavoured to ridicule and extirpate all our expectations of any future reward in another life; and secondly, they have represented it as directly incompatible with our happiness and advancement in this." Given the rejection of a future life, the motivation of a man's conduct becomes purely pragmatic. The rational lucubrations of the "projectors" of society tend to evaluate human happiness in terms of the quantity of material goods that an individual possesses and of the general prosperity of society, rather than in terms of the degree of contentment that an individual enjoys.

In the *Champion* of January 22, Fielding eschews posing a theological argument for God's existence, leaving such work to theologians like John Tillotson and Samuel Clarke. Instead, he argues for beliefs that can best advance the happiness of people at large. What possible good, he asks, can the assault of the atheist on the existence of God and the future life contribute to the happiness of the average man? On the contrary, it might have disastrous social consequences: "The ambitious, the voluptuous, the covetous, the revengeful, the malicious, steering clear of human laws only, without any fear of being called to a future account, might feast and glut their several passions with the most delicious repasts they could procure." He addresses his very considerable intellectual powers not to individual guilt, but characteristically to the impact individual acts have on society at large. He finds that those who destroy the happiness of people are the most vicious of men. Particularly culpable are those who spread their disquieting atheism and deism through the written word. From a pragmatic point of view, he asks, what would be the consequences if Dr. South is right and religion is not the mere bugbear that such writers believe it to be? "What will be the case then?" Fielding inquires, "How innocent have been the swords of the conquerors and destroyers, the heroic murderers and butchers of mankind, in comparison with a profligate pen?" Even for Hercules Vinegar this is strong language that forcefully suggests Fielding's recognition of the impact of the written word.

The Clergy

Fielding's religious views are strongly focused on the individual and society, and his lack of enthusiasm for ecclesiastical organization is revealed, not so much by direct statement as by the omission of any strong assertion of support for it. His reluctance to embrace the manifestations of organized religion, however, does not include opposition to either the role of the theologian or of the minister. Fielding speaks with respect of men like Tillotson, a member of the Anglican hierarchy, as well as well-known thinkers such as South and Barrow. He also has a high regard for the local clergyman when he acts as a man of God should. The high standards that Fielding sets for the clergy are made abundantly clear in his periodical essays.

In a series of Saturday papers in the *Champion* between March 29 and April 19, 1740, Fielding sets forth his conception of the ideal clergyman. With clear reference to the clergy, he criticizes, in the March 29 number, the tendency to condemn all members of a profession because of the shortcomings of a few; at the same time he realizes that some individuals seek immunity from criticism because of the dignity associated with their calling. Fielding's evaluation of the clergy and the efficacy of the means by which they were trained in his day is reflected in a passage of sustained irony. Numerous public schools, which are conducted by masters chosen "with proper respect to their morals as well as learning," provide students for the two great universities that are similarly noted "for their erudition, sobriety and good order." Moreover, after the strictest and most impartial examination leading to holy orders, "the young divine can afterwards expect no promotion, but from his merit, no ecclesiastical preferments being by any means whatever to be purchased." Writing toward the end of Walpole's ministry, in which politics and ecclesiastical preferment were closely interrelated, and in an era in which university life lacked both the moral training of a seminary and a uniformly high standard of intellectual study, Fielding's description of clerical preparation ironically suggests the reasons for much that he finds wrong among the clergy of his day.

The concept of the clergy developed in the Gospels is the basis for Fielding's first standard of judgment. It is curious that Fielding, whose writings turn so often to the treatment of the poor, views the clergy, not from the point of view of their role in improving the material state of the faithful, but from a more intellectually based sense of the theological mission of the disciples. Their mission, he affirms, was to convey to the people a knowledge of the truths of Christianity, and through this knowledge to provide the means to salvation. Fielding reveals an extensive knowledge of the New Testament, but, more than that, he takes a theologically traditional approach to the Christian ministry. The office of the disciples and their successors, the clergy of Fielding's time, was simply "to call or summon men into the kingdom of God, and by spreading the excellence of His doctrine to induce men to become followers of Christ, and by that means partakers of His salvation." The office of clergyman, which "concerns the eternal happiness of the souls of men," he asserts, "must be of greatly superior dignity and honour to any of those whose business is at most the regulation or well-being of the body only."

For Fielding, the first personal quality a clergyman should possess is humility, on the authority of both Christ himself and St. Paul, who advocated the same virtue, "forbidding any to think high of himself" because "very few wise, or mighty, or noble, in a worldly sense, were called to the ministry." In the *Champion* of April 5 Fielding progresses to the second characteristic of the ideal clergyman, his love of the poor which is demonstrated by charity in dealing with them. Curiously, it is not charity in the expected sense of care for the social needs of the less fortunate, but charity in the more religious sense of Paul's epistle to the Corinthians (1: 13). The charitable clergyman "suffereth long," "is not easily provoked," "beareth all things," and "endureth all things." The charitable minister, moreover, manifests a sense of forgiveness, is kind and liberal in attitude, and avoids envy and pride.

Fielding is concerned especially with the way in which the clergyman reacts to men of wealth and position. The ideal clergyman will not pass over sin and iniquity in individuals because of the power that they possess. He will not take "the wages of sinful men" nor partake "of their dainties at the expense of flattering them in their iniquity." Fielding is aware of the danger to their calling when the clergy mix the material with the spiritual. Observing in the *Champion* of April 12 that the law views the clergy in a highly respected light, and provides them with the highest honors, a large degree of immunity, and substantial revenues, Fielding focuses on the dereliction of duty by absentee clergymen. So serious is the obligation of the clergy to devote their energies to their cures, that the law provides that they must not be absent from them for extended periods. Moreover, it prohibits them from taking lands to farm or to buy and sell goods in the marketplace, so that "nothing might prevent them from discharging their duties to the souls of men."

In the last of the series of papers devoted to the clergy, that of April 19, Fielding summarizes the contents of the preceding four, bringing together his thoughts on the character of the true minister. He finds, in essence, that "a bad clergyman is the worst of men," for such a man has thoroughly studied the matters of religion and has constantly in front of him the picture of Heaven and Hell. The nature of his calling makes the clergyman aware of the brevity of this life compared with the prospect of eternal happiness, and his failure to act accordingly suggests a lack of true belief. Fielding thus links his condemnation of the unworthy man of God with his general criticism of the pretenders in society who take on false appearances to pursue unworthy ends, and thus on the surface appear good but in their hearts are corrupt.

The Poor

Fielding's perception of the society of his day, both in terms of what it was and in terms of what it should have been, is amply suggested in his essays dealing with the poor. Two papers in the *Champion,* of February 16 and 19, 1739–40, form an important summary of his views on charity as a yardstick for judging the culture of a society. After noting that each society is characterized by the particular vices or virtues then in fashion, he concludes, not as facetiously as might be suspected, that "the amiable characteristic of the present age is charity." He finds evidence of this in the great number of beggars to be found throughout the country, as well as in public manifestations of charity and efforts to care for the poor.

Proposals to deal systematically with the poor had begun during the reign of Queen Elizabeth after the monasteries and similar religious organizations no longer functioned as instruments of relieving distress. Many proposals in the eighteenth century moved in the direction of putting the poor to work, often through the establishment of public workhouses, and some of the most practical minds of the century tried to find solutions. Prominent among such thinkers were Fielding and Daniel Defoe.[3] The difficulty with workhouses as a means of ending the ravages of poverty was as Defoe suggested that, in engaging the poor to manufacture products in competition with the efforts of the working class, each poor man tended to displace an individual who was supporting himself without public assistance. Defoe's observations were not characteristic of the spirit of the age, however, and the views of John Locke formed an inspiration for those seeking practical solutions. The basic thrust of Locke's social philosophy called attention to the obligation of each individual to contribute to the society of which he is a member, rather than to the duty of society to minister to the needs of the individual. Among those proposals offered by Locke in his *Report of the Board of Trade to the Lords Justices respecting the Relief and Employment of the Poor* (1697) were plans for the impressment of the begging poor into the navy and the commitment of older men to three years of hard labor in houses of correction. Similar proposals were offered for women and for boys and girls under the age of fourteen. Even in the cases of those who, for reasons of health, were unable to work, he hoped to offset the cost of their maintenance by providing them with partial employment.

Fielding's most direct and practical approach to the problem is found in his *Proposal for Making an Effectual Provision for the Poor,* in which he offers detailed plans for the construction of a workhouse where the poor might be gainfully employed. Repugnant as the workhouse idea is to modern society, its practicality in the eighteenth century is indicated by the fact that many of the poor lacked even a place to sleep. Moreover, costly efforts to care for the poor through other means had not brought them actual relief. In 1756 a committee of the House of Commons estimated that poor relief cost one and one-half million pounds a year. Although Fielding's estimate of such costs in his *Proposal* is somewhat less, he supports the view that the methods previously taken have not really helped the poor: "For while a million yearly is raised . . . many . . . are . . . starved; many more languish in want and misery; of the rest, numbers are found begging or pilfering in the streets to-day, and to-morrow are locked in gaols and bridewells."[4] Fielding's solution is to provide a very large center for the poor, so that the advantages of size may be used both to reduce the cost of administration and to provide more varied work to employ many different abilities. "The expense and difficulty of carrying this purpose into execution will always increase in proportion to the smallness of the body of people by whose hands it is to be executed. And this is the reason why work-houses (more properly called idle-houses) have by experience been found to produce no better effect: for if the masters of these houses had a real disposition to set the poor to work, and if they had all adequate capacities for that purpose, they would by no means be able to effect it."[5]

Although Fielding characteristically seeks practical ways by which society can function as a whole, he is aware of the importance of individual responsibility. This is particularly significant in the dispensing of charity. A charitable individual may err when he avoids publicity, and thus makes charitable donations seem to be something to be avoided rather than pointed to with pride. On the other hand, begging is often an effort to avoid contributing, through work, to the social structure. Fielding's orientation toward advocating that which makes society function well leads him to criticize those who, to a modern sociologist, would be most deserving of help, the begging poor.

Fielding is convinced that many of those who beg do so as a substitute for work. Beggars, he observes in the *Champion* of February 16 "deserve punishment more than relief, and are a shame not to the legislative but the executive power of our laws." His seemingly callous attitude toward the poor appears less severe if considered in the context of his preoccupation with making society work. Whether a man is willing to work or not, and the extent to which he is himself responsible for his situation, weighs heavily with the novelist. In a significant passage in the same essay, he points out as worthy of charity those born to circumstances of genteel life, who have been well educated and who, through no fault of their own, find themselves both without resources and without training for an occupation through which they might make a living. His sympathy is for those victimized by society and especially for educated persons who are deprived of the normal and appropriate means of supporting themselves and their families. Fielding's is not an egalitarian view and is much in step with the stratified society in which he lived. The poor, whatever the cause of their condition, need that which will enable them to maintain in dignity their particular place in the social structure. Thus, those born to the higher levels of society have a claim to the kind of sustenance that will enable them to maintain their appropriate place in the hierarchy.

Curiously, Fielding finds the extravagant dissipation of one's estate to be more deserving of pity than of condemnation: "I look on indiscretion with pity, not abhorrence, and on no indiscretion with so much pity as that of extravagance, which as it may bring men into the greatest calamities of this life; so it may arise from the goodness, the openness, and the generosity of the heart." In the eighteenth century the final outcome for such individuals was often debtor's prison. Sympathetic as Fielding is to this type of poor, he is not unmindful that the reason for their distress is their failure to come to grips with changed conditions. In most cases, a desire to live a life beyond a person's financial capabilities accounts for his difficulties, and reflecting on this fact leads Fielding to one of his major concerns, the tendency of mankind to value appearance more than reality, to desire to appear more affluent than one is.

Fielding's next *Champion,* on February 19, 1739–40, contains a discussion of the desire for luxury and how it tempts individuals to spend beyond their capabilities. But the lure of luxury and the temptation to extravagance are not the only sources of the social imbalance that brings members of the middle-class to a poverty level. The structure of the society and the conditions under which it functions contribute to the problem. The practice of leaving estates to the eldest brother and trusting the care of younger children to his charge often does not work, for characteristically the younger children of families of position are not trained to earn their livings by trade or profession. Although careers in the military and the church are open to them, influence and interest are usually needed for success and are often not available. Lamentably, birth, education, and capacity are often ignored in the passing out of places, and Fielding's desires in this respect are more idealistic than achievable. "I hope," he writes, "particularly, that it will be no objection to any one of merit that his family is poor, and has no interest, circumstances which should rather produce charity than restrain it; and any person or persons, who, by a contrary preceding, are the cause of innumerable distresses in gentlemen's families, make a very bad amends for their behaviour by scattering a few pieces among the mob."

Fielding's hard-headed view of society is supported by his moral conviction that social pretentiousness and following "whim, fancy, fashion and pride" have serious economic ramifications and often deter industrious individuals from supporting themselves. He is much ahead of his century in understanding the need to help small businesses to flourish. For Fielding, the support of the rich tradesman merely because of his "name" is a social fault, but, unfortunately, people are willing to pay a premium for a "name": "Do we not every day confess that we give advanced prices for the names of particular tradesmen who have the assurance to exact larger prices for their commodities than their brethren, only because they are richer, and might consequently afford to sell cheaper?" Such tradesmen do not benefit society when they fail to reduce the cost of goods, but society itself is also at fault, since it does not support less affluent but needy tradesmen merely because of social pretense.

The last category of needy poor, and those who perhaps suffer the greatest distress, is that of people imprisoned for debts which they cannot pay. Debtors' prisons are for Fielding "a shocking reflection" on his society both because of the suffering they cause, and because they deprive the nation of the industry of its people. "How agreeable," he observes ironically, "the making such numbers of subjects not only useless to, but a burden on the community, may be to a wise or a polite nation, or the inflicting such misery on so many for sometimes no offence, may be to a humane or a Christian people, I will not determine."

When Fielding returns to the subject of charity in the *Covent Garden Journal* of June 2, 1752, he expands his previously developed views through a discussion of public charity, with particular emphasis on those who will their money to either the Church or public hospitals. Fielding sharply attacks the practice of giving money to the Church as a form of charity: "Thus the unwilling Will, as Dr. Barrow pleasantly calls it, was at last signed. The fruits of fraud and rapine were trusted to the use of the Church, and the greatest rascals died very good saints, and their memories were consecrated to honour and good example." He condemns the practice, not only as the product of fear and vanity and without any benevolent inspiration, but also as a significant social injustice that defrauds one's heirs of their rightful inheritance. Willing one's estate to public charitable institutions is equally offensive: "Henceforward, instead of robbing their relations for the use of the Church, a method was devised of robbing them for the use of the poor." It was in this way that "poor-houses, alms-houses, colleges, and hospitals" began to appear in England. Although Fielding had expressed himself in favor of the formation of the foundling hospital in the *Champion* of February 21, 1739–40, and again at the conclusion of the *Covent Garden Journal* essay, he distrusts privately endowed public institutions and is aware of the corruption that almost inevitably creeps into them: "If a man hath lived any time in the world, he must have observed such horrid and notorious abuses of all public charities, that he must be convinced (with a very few exceptions) that he will do no manner of good by contributing to them." He is aware that many seemingly charitable institutions are not readily available, on a nondiscriminatory basis, to those who are most in need of them, and he condemns "all hospitals whatever, where it is a matter of favour to get a patient admitted, and where the forms of admission are so troublesome and tedious, that the properest objects (those I mean who are most wretched and friendless) may as well aspire at a place at court as at a place in the hospital." Not objecting to public charity as such, he deplores public charity that does not serve the truly needy poor and consistently judges the efficacy of a particular form of charity on the basis of its social utility. He thus exempts from his criticism both the foundling hospital and the hospital "for the accommodation of poor women in their lying-in."

Political Thought

Understanding Fielding's political thought can be obscured by an undue emphasis on his opposition to the Walpole ministry and his satire directed against it in both his dramas and *Jonathan Wild*. Fielding's two poems addressed to Walpole, one in 1730 and the other a year later, are generally not regarded as serious attempts to obtain the favor of the minister. On the other hand, they are not antagonistic and might have earned consideration from a man more sympathetic to the arts than Walpole. Within the poems, moreover, can be recognized the seeds of Fielding's subsequent satiric attacks, for they contain little praise but a forthright recognition of the minister's power to grant places and dispense favors. Fielding's opposition to Walpole recognized the opportunities for corruption inherent in the office of the prime minister and the manner in which Walpole took advantage of his office. Fielding was not a narrow partisan, nor was he opposed to the political structure as such. He strongly supported his close friend, Henry Pelham, and his government, and he comments favorably on his old enemy, Walpole, in the *Journal of a Voyage to Lisbon*.[6]

Fielding's political philosophy centered on support of the Hanoverian, George II, partly because of his sense of tradition in British government, but also out of fear that the return of the Stuart dynasty would adversely affect British freedom. He frequently expresses anti-Jacobin sentiments out of concern that the throne in the hands of the successors of Charles II would result in an influence on the government of papal authority and of the political interests of Catholic France and Spain.

Fielding accepts the traditional concept of the three estates of the realm, King, Lords, and Commons. He is also aware of the power of the "mob" which he chooses to regard as a "fourth estate." Of major concern to Fielding is the office of prime minister as developed and exploited by Walpole. In the *Champion* of May 8, 1740, Fielding comments on the ability of one man to maneuver the workings of government so as to dominate the actions of an entire nation, thus assuming to himself the power traditionally reserved to the three estates. A distortion of the normal functioning of government results when a single individual learns to manipulate the system to his own advantage. This Fielding felt Walpole had accomplished and had, consequently, usurped functions not intended for his use in the established political system. The nature of the office of prime minister, the highest reward of the "great political cause between *Woodall Out and Takeall In,*"[7] risks the venality of a particular incumbent. Fielding could appropriately attack Walpole when he was minister and later support Pelham in the same position, for he believed that one had exceeded the normal limits of his office and the other had not.

Fielding's sense of the body politic recognized that the nation depends for its protection on three great resources, the House of Commons, the King, and God. The Commons is the protector of English "liberties and properties," but if unfit representatives are elected, who "should openly support a minister in barefaced iniquity," there is recourse to the King to whom the people have "a right to apply for redress." Finally, if all human things fail, appeal may be made "to our Father in Heaven." Fielding links the final welfare of the people to providential intervention, for God "hath more than once interposed His divine hand and saved His People."

The naturally corruptive nature of politics explains Fielding's lack of involvement with political parties. Often facetiously and with penetrating wit, Fielding notes the pattern of assault that politics makes on the moral fiber of the people. Under the guise of a letter "To the Citizens of London" in the *Champion* of December 18, 1739, Fielding laments the misuse of the election process. The important protection available to the city of London through free elections is often frustrated when the promises of politicians corrupt the people into electing those unworthy to serve. Ironically, Fielding protests that this will never be the case, for "Who can believe that the city of London will submit to be bribed? Will stoop to low, mean, and pitiful bribes?" The ballot is the means by which the citizens can stem the tide of corruption, or participate in it.

The nature of man explains for Fielding the evolution of the political world. His *Essay on the Knowledge of the Characters of Men* emphasizes his familiar theme of dissimulation and deceit. The natural tendency in that direction is "nourished and improved" by the education of men, for men are taught "to conceal vices," rather than "to cultivate virtues." Politicians have developed the "Art of thriving." This art, which "points out to every individual his own particular and separate advantage, to which he is to sacrifice the interest of all others," ultimately constitutes the "Art of Politics."[8]

Although Fielding's ideas seem more clearly associated with the Whig position than the Tory, he was not committed to political partisanship, but to serving the needs of his society. His dedication to this ideal is expressed in his social pamphlets, his work as a magistrate, and his development of the Universal Register Office. He seems not to have viewed political pressure and political alliances as an effective means of achieving social improvement. Party seemed less important than men. Fielding's ability to work within a political structure is demonstrated by the submission of his *Proposal* for poor-law legislation to the Pelham administration, but, for the most part, he avoided narrow political partisanship, particularly in his periodical essays.

Although Fielding's vigorous attack on the Jacobites and others supporting the cause of Prince Charles in 1745 might be seen as an exception to his usual stand, his efforts in the cause of the existing government were patriotic in their intent, and not truly partisan. Although extreme Tories might have been expected to welcome a return of the Stuart dynasty, support of Prince Charles was seen by others as little more than support of a foreign intrusion on the British system of government, and the issue was not recognized as a truly partisan one. For Fielding, the revolution was a genuine threat to the peace of the nation that posed dangerous long-range consequences if it succeeded. In the first issue of the *True Patriot* he asserts his avoidance of partisanship unequivocally, "I am of no party; a word which I hope, by these my labours, to eradicate out of our constitution; this being the true source of all those evils which we have reason to complain of." He maintains this position both in the remaining issues of the *True Patriot* and in those of the *Jacobite's Journal*.

In the *Champion* of February 14, 1739–40, Fielding has Hercules Vinegar respond to those who seek his support for a variety of political positions. He finds politics adequately discussed in the *Gazetteer*, which often finds its best use in the service of the privy, and he declares: "I find I am no politician." Rejecting those who see the origin of politics in the devil, or Pandora's box, he favors the theory that "it came first into the world at the building of Babel," for those who attempted to build that tower were pursuing an objective "bearing an exact resemblance to most political schemes." Finally, he hopes that his correspondents will no longer ask him to satisfy their political questions, assuring them that he knows "nothing of the matter."

Fielding desires to avoid the kind of personal slander and calumny often associated with political writing and in his periodicals often condemns this vice as a destroyer of reputation. In the *Champion* of March 6, 1739–40, he finds that slander frequently arises from a desire for revenge, and very often out of a spirit of malice. He suggests how to deal with material aimed at the destruction of reputations:

My advice to him who hears a scandalous story is to suppress it, at least until he is certain of its truth; and even then he would do well to weigh the guilt of it with candour, and to examine whether any good consequences to others will attend the discovery. A scandalous story should be heard with reluctance, believed with difficulty, and published with deliberation: . . . When we have once set forth the calumny, we can recall it no more, nor can we ever make any amends to the injured party, if we are mistaken; the tongue of the slanderer being like the sword of the murderer, and the loss of reputation almost as irretrievable as that of life.

Politics along with literary rivalry frequently evoked slander of a most personal sort in the eighteenth century. That Fielding himself was not always without fault in this regard is seen in his attacks on Cibber, Conyers Middleton, Walpole, and lesser enemies. Most of Fielding's excursions into personal satire, however, were against figures already targeted by others, and in most instances he was capitalizing on already established bases for his satire. It is the revelation of hidden facts or the circulation of false or unsupported stories that he primarily condemns, and such material has characteristically been the staple of political assault.

Fielding's political writing was in support of the nation, the established form of government, and the preservation of good order. In this he continued the train of thinking that established his social conscience. He saw much of life in terms of solving the problems of living, and his practical intelligence was activated by social concern. As magistrate, he established what ultimately became the first police force of London; his pamphlets on crime and on other social questions offered practical solutions to the difficulties confronting society, and his highly successful Universal Register Office served the needs of the people in finding employment, securing insurance, and in providing for the exchange of goods, both stolen and found.

The stratified society that existed at the heart of London life in the eighteenth century left little room for what now would be called upward social mobility. Fielding completely accepted the existing structure and within its framework addressed the question of how to provide people with a means of achieving happiness and justice. Although he had little sympathy for the begging poor, or for those who deliberately withheld their labor from the community, and, following Locke, held useful labor to be the duty and obligation of all, his ideas were essentially Christian in both their origin and development. He was a supporter of the institution of the clergy and the presence of the Church, but he had little admiration for ecclesiastical organization or complex theological doctrine. He saw the nature of man optimistically and valued natural, benevolent instincts. Theological and philosophical speculation, with which he was familiar in some detail, were less important in his hierarchy of values than benevolent good nature in forming the good Christian, in satisfying the individual's duty to God, and in preparing for a future life. At base, Fielding's thought emerges out of a traditional Christian temperament and finds expression in practical social approaches.

Chapter Three
Experiments in Prose Fiction

When the Walpole ministry succeeded in having the Licensing Act passed by Parliament on June 21, 1737, it not only succeeded in having all plays licensed, but it also closed all but the two patent theaters, Drury Lane and Covent Garden.[1] Fielding's Little Theatre in the Haymarket was unable to continue to operate. What Fielding had taught Walpole and other astute politicians was that the visual media provided a power very different from that of the written word. The ability to influence great numbers of people at the same time, not through the logic or even the distortion of logic possible through the written word, but through the simultaneous force of the presentation of ideas and the forensic power of the spoken word had been demonstrated by Fielding. The mass psychology that could be appealed to in the theater was an immediate threat that could not be ignored. There was no refuting the powerful voice of the dramatic artist, for the response, if it were to be made through the same vehicle, would take time and comparable dramatic ability. It also became evident that the ability of Fielding's theater to attack through the caustic humor and brilliant irony of farce was not matched by comparable ability on the part of the government to defend itself. Inevitably, defending a cause in the theater was considerably duller than attacking the party in power.

The closing of the theaters was directed not primarily against Fielding as a person, but against his theater, which had become a source of satirical criticism, and against the political power that the theater had demonstrated itself capable of exercising. In a response made to Fielding's comedy, *The Historical Register for the Year 1736,* in the ministry's publication *The Daily Gazetteer,* a distinction was made between the press and the theater as vehicles for attack on government. Clearly the press, through ministry-supported newspapers, could influence public opinion on an equal footing with those of the opposition, but a similar equality was impossible in the theater. The Licensing Act, therefore, was designed to bring to an end the particular theatrical adventures in political satire and farce that Fielding had developed to a fine art. He could have returned to producing conventional dramas, but functioning as a theatrical person in the political arena was Fielding's forte. With characteristic practicality, Fielding decided to undertake training in the law as well as to write in nondramatic forms. He began reading law in the Middle Temple in 1737 and within three years had completed the usual six-or-seven-year course of study. He was called to the bar and began active work as a lawyer on June 20, 1740. Because Fielding did not achieve immediate or great success as a barrister, he found writing to be an essential supplement to his income. Even after being made Justice of the Peace for Westminster in October, 1748, he continued his literary efforts.

While still studying law, Fielding began his work on the *Champion* and in its pages experimented with a variety of literary formats. He demonstrated that his greatest strength was humor, transmitted largely through irony. His wide reading in both classical and modern literature provided a strong basis for establishing intellectual contact with his reader, whom he drew into his confidence on the fictitious assurance that the reader shared with him a wealth of literary and real experience that enabled them together to grasp the intellectual irony of life.

Through the fictitious author of the *Champion,* Hercules Vinegar, and his family, Fielding establishes the kind of intimate relationship between reader and writer that he subsequently achieves in his novels. For example, Vinegar's son, Jack, who "wears fine clothes, and keeps the best company" witnesses the scene of the unhappy rich where gambling and family disputes are a way of life. Characteristically, Fielding focuses on food and eating as the focal point of contrast. The meal of the rich is punctuated, despite its luxury, with disagreements and complaints, whereas the meal, witnessed by Hercules himself, at the home of a country clergyman is of a much more humble sort, but is consumed "with the utmost cheerfulness" (February 26, 1739–40). In thus drawing the reader into a sense of intimacy as an experienced fellow adventurer in life, the moral truth of his view becomes overwhelmingly persuasive.

For Fielding, however, the periodical possessed serious limitations that inevitably prevented his fully expressing his artistic and aesthetic vision through it. Although it is possible to derive, in the sum total of the essays in the *Champion,* a fairly complete sense of Fielding's social and moral outlook, what emerges has the ultimate incompleteness, from an aesthetic point of view, of all forms of didactic expression. Fictitious scenes become illustrative of social, political, or moral principles instead of conveying the fused sense of reality that great art can achieve. Probably spurred by the

success of Samuel Richardson's first novel, *Pamela,* Fielding experimented
in the space of only a few years with four different types of fiction, each of
which reveals a complex interest in form. *Shamela* (April, 1741), *Joseph
Andrews* (February, 1742), and both *A Journey from This World to the Next*
and *Jonathan Wild (The Miscellanies,* April, 1743) emerge from the same
period of experimentation.

Shamela

Fielding's experiments with fiction in the *Champion,* along with other
efforts at creative prose, provide evidence that Fielding would have been a
novelist had Samuel Richardson never written *Pamela,* but it is equally
clear that *Joseph Andrews,* Fielding's first masterpiece in the genre, would
not have taken the shape it had without the previous appearance of his own
Shamela, [2] which could not have been written had it not been for
Richardson's first novel. *Shamela* is not a novel as such; rather, it is a
brilliant spoof of *Pamela* and an attack on the human pretense that parades
tawdry motives behind the appearance of virtue. It dissects the vicious
vanity that motivates people to appear in the moral habit that society
demands, while using it to perpetuate vices that society tolerates.

Richardson's *Pamela* was published anonymously in January, 1741, in
two volumes and went through four editions by May of that year. In
December, two additional volumes, *Pamela in her Exalted Condition,* were
added. The novel became the talk of the town as it met with immediate
and great success, due partly to the gossipy effect achieved by the novelist's
use of the letter format, partly to the titillation of the reader by the
psychological analysis of Pamela's sexual motivation supported by explicit
scenes of love, and partly to the parading of the novel as an epitome of
moral instruction.

Richardson's story is of a young servant girl who, upon the death of her
mistress, is left in the household of the son of her former employer, a
wealthy young squire who subjects her to amorous advances. Pamela
steadfastly resists the erotic approaches of Mr. B——, as he is called, despite
the efforts of her fellow servant, Mrs. Jewkes, who allies herself with their
master. Pamela survives her abduction to Mr. B——'s country estate and not
only preserves her virtue, but also receives a proposal of marriage from Mr.
B——. In her efforts, she is supported by a model clergyman friend, Parson
Williams, and by the morally correct and prudent advice of her parents.

Literary imitation and parody assumed the proportion of a major genre
in the eighteenth century and was practiced in many forms, such as

Alexander Pope's poetic use of epic convention in *The Rape of the Lock* and the *Dunciad,* and Johnson's more restrictive adaptation of Juvenal in *London* and the *Vanity of Human Wishes.* In the theater, Fielding himself had mocked the heroic play in *Tom Thumb,* and Gay the conventions of Italian opera in *The Beggar's Opera.*

Fielding was not the only author to recognize the suitability of *Pamela* for literary parody, and somewhere between a dozen and a score of literary takeoffs on *Pamela* appeared in rapid succession.[3] His was by far the best.

On one level, *Shamela* parodies the letter format of Richardson's novel, creating a roundly funny version of the novelist's serious moral tale in broadly exuberant sexual comedy. What is attacked most effectively is that which formed the vital strength of Richardson's fiction, the close dissection of Pamela's motives for her actions and the tortured moral dilemma that her position in the household of Mr. B—— posed for her. In letters that purport to be the newly discovered real letters of Shamela, that is, Pamela, who had changed her name in the letters Richardson supposedly edited, her motives are revealed to be tawdry, dishonest, but strongly and successfully pragmatic. Shamela is not the innocent girl she seemed to be in the guise of Pamela, who struggled hard to avoid the immoral overtures of Mr. B—— only to find herself successfully in love with him, and capable of achieving, in the most orthodox sentimental fashion of the day, the reform of her master through his perception of the true depths of her virtue. Rather, Shamela is a designing female who has already mothered an illegitimate child by Parson Williams and who, parading as Pamela, skillfully manipulates Mr. B—— into marriage, not for reasons of sentimental love, but for pragmatic motives of worldly success. Fielding thus reverses the moral foundation of the novel through a different analysis and separation of the motives of its heroine. Fielding's spoof went to the very heart of Richardson's conception of the novel and demonstrated how ridicule and irony could be employed to expose vicious and indecent motives parading under the mask of virtuous deeds.

Whether or not Richardson was the recognized target of Fielding's parody cannot be ascertained with absolute certitude. F. Homes Dudden offers the improbable theory that Fielding believed Colley Cibber to be the true author of *Pamela,*[4] but it is unlikely that Fielding would conclude that the stylistically awkward author of Cibber's *Apology* had composed the *tour de force* that is *Pamela.* Although *Pamela* was published anonymously, it is clear that friends of Richardson knew of his authorship of the novel, and if friends, then why not enemies or apparent enemies? Richardson had been for years the printer of Walpole's newspaper, the *Daily Gazetteer,* an

organ in bitter opposition to Fielding's *Champion.* Although political
rivalry may account partially for the attack on *Pamela,* Fielding's main
motivation seems to have been his reaction to the theme and moral
approach of the novel.

Pamela and its author were not the only objects attacked by Fielding's
spoof. Two other prominent writers of the day shared the honor, along with
a major figure of the political nobility, Lord Hervey. Colley Cibber, the
final hero of Pope's *Dunciad* and the butt of Fielding's pen in *The Author's
Farce,* was not a surprising victim. He was fair game for literary attack as
an undistinguished poet laureate and had further incurred Fielding's
disapproval through his public defense of the Licensing Act. Conyers
Middleton, on the other hand, was a less likely victim, for as a relatively
obscure Cambridge University senior he would hardly be worth Fielding's
trouble. He might even have endeared himself to a neo-Scriblerian like
Fielding as a result of his unrelenting attacks on Pope's enemy the
Cambridge scholar, Richard Bentley, that contributed to Bentley's ouster
as master of Trinity College. But Fielding had noted that Middleton's *Life
of Cicero* was dedicated to Lord Hervey, an old and bitter enemy, and he
recognized in that dedication a model to be mocked.

Fielding parodies both the form and substance of *Pamela* with telling
effect, combining his attack on Richardson with his thrusts at Cibber and
Middleton, beginning with the title page. He alters the title to read *An
Apology for the Life of Mrs. Shamela Andrews,* thus calling attention to
Cibber's recently published *Apology* for his own life, and he unites in the
name of the fictitious author of the work, Mr. Conny Keyber, the
beginning of Cornelius Middleton with the end of Colley Cibber.

Eighteenth-century readers would not have missed, moreover, the
connotations contained in the word, Conny, still recognizable then as
meaning a dupe or cheat. This is very much what Fielding saw *Pamela* to
be. The title page boasts that *Shamela* is a book "In which, the many
notorious Falshoods and Misrepresentations of a Book called *Pamela,* Are
exposed and refuted; and all the matchless Arts of that young Politician,
set in a true and just Light." The dedication of the book is to "Fanny," the
name given to Hervey by Pope in his imitations of Horace's *Satires,* and it
is a close parody that serves to ridicule the extensive dedication of
Middleton's *Cicero* to Hervey. Two letters mock the letters puffing *Pamela*
that appeared in the second edition of that novel. Moreover, Fielding
focuses on the letter format itself by having the exchange of letters between
Parson Tickletext and Parson Oliver explain how wrong the current
evaluation of *Pamela* is and where the real truth lies. To demonstrate this,

Oliver conveys to his correspondent the authentic letters written by Shamela.

The two parsons' exchange of letters also serves to introduce the moral questions inherent in *Pamela*. Pamela's motives, though explicitly stated in the strongest moral terms, are advanced through action that casts suspicion on their sincerity. All of the explanations of the reasons why Pamela acts are her own, and Fielding demonstrates that the same actions, explained through different, less guarded letters, can lead to different conclusions. The character of Parson Williams is similarly ambivalent, and in *Shamela* his motives for action reveal a distorted religious sensibility. Faith without good works, or more specifically as an excuse for evil deeds, characterizes the moral position of Parson Williams and the advice he gives Shamela in Fielding's spoof. In treating Williams in this way, Fielding extends the range of his satire beyond Richardson's novel to embrace general religious attitudes. Williams's efforts to seduce Shamela by submerging her religious scruples depend on his convincing her that faith and prayer are more important yardsticks by which to judge the individual than the morality of his acts. Largely as a result of the way Parson Williams is presented, *Shamela* becomes a major attack on hypocrisy in religion as practiced by Fielding's contemporaries, including the clergy.

Good works and proper motivation are inseparable from faith in Fielding's view of religion. In his apostrophe to the "Little book, charming *Pamela,*" Parson Tickletext demonstrates the moral inadequacy of his reading of the novel: "Dost thou not teach us to pray, to sing Psalms, and to honour the Clergy? Are not these the whole Duty of Man?" Echoing as he does one of the truly important spiritual books of the seventeenth century, Fielding points out the inversion of the values advanced by such works in the conduct of the people of his day. Such a view has little to do with Richardson's novel, but a great deal to do with the way society, and the clergy, reacted to it.

Fielding is careful to have Shamela use her assumed name, Pamela, in all her dealings with Mr. B--, whose name is filled out to Booby. The Squire does not know of her true background, nor does he suspect her prior involvement with Parson Williams, who shares in the fraudulent pretense inherent in the heroine's change of name.

The close parallel that exists between the novel and the spoof is the source of much entertainment in the reading of *Shamela*. Fielding has Shamela write exceedingly well, thus echoing the ability that she demonstrates in Richardson's novel. He is careful not to destroy the identities of

Richardson's main characters while he succeeds in impugning their motives. Booby becomes far less important than Williams as their relationships with the heroine are revised. As *Shamela* focuses on the immorality of their conduct, the tawdry actions in Richardson's novel are remembered, suggesting the absurdity of the use of *Pamela* as a basis for moral instruction.

The intellectual thrust of *Shamela* is a study of the relationship between religion and conduct and between spirit and matter. These relationships are effectively demonstrated through Fielding's juxtaposition of action and motive. Shamela has been well schooled in the pragmatism of Williams as she prepares for Squire Booby, just arrived in a coach and six: "I immediately run up into my Room, and stript, and washed, and drest myself as well as I could, and put on my prettiest round-ear'd Cap, and pulled down my Stays, to show as much as I could of my Bosom, (for Parson *Williams* says, that is the most beautiful part of a Woman), and then I practised over all my Airs before the Glass, and then I sat down and read a Chapter in The Whole Duty of Man" (Letter 10). The ironic juxtaposition of the title of the popular seventeenth-century devotional work with the worldly actions of Pamela reveals her complete confusion of values under the religious instruction of Parson Williams.

Fielding feared the emotional preaching of the Methodists that triggered the sudden reformation of sinful lives. His belief that true Christianity required man to act with consideration toward other human beings conflicted with the notion of sudden and probably unreliable repentance. Shamela describes for her mother one of the sermons of Parson Williams and the easy doctrine it advocates:

"Well, on *Sunday* Parson *Williams* came, according to his Promise, and an excellent Sermon he preached; his Text was, *Be not Righteous over-much*; and, indeed, he handled it in a very fine way; he showed us that the Bible doth not require too much Goodness of us, and that People very often call things Goodness that are not so. That to go to Church, and to pray, and to sing Psalms, and to honour the Clergy, and to repent, is true Religion; and 'tis not doing good to one another, for that is one of the greatest Sins we can commit, when we don't do it for the sake of Religion." (Letter 9)

Shamela's words touch the nub of the controversy, the tendency to confuse motive with action when judging the morality of an act, and the further tendency to place the main weight on motive.

Through Williams and his instruction of Shamela, we have an emblematic representation of dishonest motivation diguised beneath the mask of virtue and social acceptance that is the way of the world and that is also the basis, as Fielding sees it, for the actions of Richardson's heroine. By a brilliant leap, Fielding has demonstrated that the popular acceptance of the surface morality of Richardson's novel and the exaggerated extolling of its instructional value reveal the shortcomings of the age's vision of Christianity, and he thus links the instructional use of religion by Parson Williams to the instructional use of *Pamela* by the clergy of the day.

Joseph Andrews

The publication of *Joseph Andrews* made it clear that Fielding was committed to prose fiction of a highly artistic sort, and that he had seriously investigated a variety of formats whereby his conception of life could be revealed. *Don Quixote* had suggested to him how the wisdom of the addled hero of Cervantes could be used to shape the character of Parson Adams, whose preoccupation with Christian charity diminishes his practical sense, and whose bookishness distorts his perspective on the world about him. Paramount in Fielding's thinking, moreover, was the realistic fiction of the French picaresque writers, Scarron, LeSage, and Marivaux, in whose work acute observation of life supported the comic spirit. Perhaps most important was Fielding's sense of the epic as the model for great fiction, and he hit upon the idea of creating a prose epic that was suited to comedy rather than to the heroic themes of its classical models.[5]

Fielding's expression of reality is consistently comic, but his fundamental views are essentially serious. Following Aristotle's distinction between comedy and tragedy in the drama, he notes that the comic epic in prose is related to the serious epic in a manner similar to the relationship between comedy and tragedy in the drama. He distinguishes in the "Preface" between romances, which contain "very little instruction or entertainment," and the "comic romance" or "comic epic-poem in prose," a genre he is introducing for the first time in English. "It differs from the serious romance," he points out, "in its fable and action, in this: that as in the one these are grave and solemn, so in the other they are light and ridiculous: it differs in its characters by introducing persons of inferior rank, and consequently, of inferior manners, whereas the grave romance sets the highest before us: lastly, in its sentiments and diction, by preserving the ludicrous instead of the sublime."

The "Preface" develops in some detail Fielding's sense of what he is attempting in the novel. He rejects burlesque as the basis for comedy, quoting Shaftesbury to the effect that burlesque is not to be found among the works of the ancients. Furthermore, he rejects the use of most forms of caricature, using as a model comic history painting which avoids scenes common in caricature in which "all distortions and exaggerations whatever are" acceptable. Only in language might the burlesque be admitted, and his work will be devoted to the ridiculous, the true source of which he finds in affectation.

For Fielding, the significant vices present in the society of his day, and recognizable in *Pamela,* are related to affectation. In increasingly frequent and serious ways he devotes his work to the revelation of the shams of life, the pretenses and frauds, both petty and of consequence, which have come to characterize life. The clergyman, the lawyer, the statesman, as well as persons of more ordinary occupation share a common tendency toward pretense. This affectation is the source of the truly comic, which is, therefore, not merely or even primarily directed toward laughter for its own sake, but toward presenting a profound comment on human existence, by stripping away the mask of pretense and revealing the actions of men for what they truly are. This he accomplished in *Shamela* as he had previously done in the drama and in the pages of the *Champion.* But his plans for the novel, outlined in the "Preface," suggest that the work will create a greater fusion of artistic method and intellectual objective than he has previously achieved. In looking for a way to exploit the genre of prose fiction brought to the fore by Richardson, Fielding provides a significant analysis of that which is comic in life, and how it can best be treated artistically.

In examining the source of the ridiculous as affectation, Fielding recognizes both amiable and vicious manifestations of it. He sees affectation as proceeding from either vanity or hypocrisy, with vanity producing the less serious consequences. While this concept is not new to Fielding's work, his recognizing its suitability for the subject matter of the comic romance is extremely important. Vanity may lead to rather modest peccadillos, such as those expressed through the character of Parson Adams, whose vanity leads him to believe his sermons to be of greater value than they are; but hypocrisy leads to serious vices by persuading its victims to hide their vices under the cloak of corresponding virtues. The motivations are substantially different: vanity resulting from wishing merely to purchase applause by putting on false colors; hypocrisy emanating from an individual's desire to avoid censure, often for serious faults, by deceiving others into believing vice to be virtue.

Finally, Fielding explains the necessary introduction of serious vices into his novel, observing: "first, that it is very difficult to pursue a series of human actions, and keep clear from them. Secondly, that the vices to be found here are rather the accidental consequences of some human frailty or foible, than causes habitually existing in the mind. Thirdly, that they are never set forth as the objects of ridicule, but detestation. Fourthly, that they are never the principal figure at that time on the scene; and, lastly, they never produce the intended evil." He concludes by asserting that the work is not aimed at particular individuals, and that he has been careful to mask the identity of those who have served as his models.

The theory of the comic epic in prose outlined in Fielding's "Preface" is reinforced by other observations on his art in the introductory chapters of the first three books of the novel. In the first he alerts the reader to the irony inherent in a work that proclaims itself a history on its title page but that greatly differs from conventional history. His concept of biography, as an extension of history applied to the lives of individual people, is concerned less with a recitation of facts than with the moral significance of particular actions. In the second book, Fielding explains that the work is divided into books and chapters to provide the reader with an opportunity to reflect on what he has read. Finally, in the third, he provides a detailed discussion of biography as history, concluding that true history is that kind of biography, such as Cervantes's *Don Quixote,* in which the fundamental reality of what is related is true although the particular time and place may be fictitious. The readers of *Joseph Andrews* will "know the lawyer in the stage-coach the moment they hear his voice," for the book describes "not men but manners; not an individual, but a species" (bk. 3, chap. 1). In this sense the dominant passions of individual characters in the novel become representative of characteristics of human behavior that may be found in persons in all occupations in any century.

Fielding succeeds admirably in exploiting his notion of the comic epic in prose, both in the form and content of *Joseph Andrews.* Fully aware of the epic as his model, he employs devices of the genre, both in minor ways, such as the use of extended similes, and in more extensive sections, such as the introduction of parodies of epic battles. Of most importance, he provides a logical structure by dividing the work into four books and numerous chapters. His hero is in motion during much of the novel, traveling with his companion, Parson Adams, from London to the country seat of Lady Booby. The work is constructed symmetrically, with most of the first book devoted to Joseph's encounter with Lady Booby, the two middle books to his and Parson Adams's adventures on the road, and the last, balancing the first book, to a confrontation with Lady Booby at her country seat.

Within this design, and forming an integral part of the work, are two major digressions in the form of stories told to the travelers on their journey, digressions that serve to reinforce the thematic thrust of the main narrative and, at the same time, strengthen the delineation of the character of Parson Adams through the revelation of his gossipy penchant for romantic tales.[6] "The History of Leonora or the Unfortunate Jilt" serves not only as a story of misplaced pragmatism in marriage, as Leonora gives up Horatio, the young man she truly loves, and with him a life of modestly affluent happiness, for the glamor of the glittering Bellarmine and his coach and six, but also as counterpoint, at the end of the novel, to Fanny's rejection of the similar glitter of Beau Didapper. The second digression, Mr. Wilson's story of the temptations of the town, his early susceptibility to them, and his eventual happiness found in moderation, contrasts with the life offered Joseph by Lady Booby and the humble existence of Parson Adams. It also provides, at the middle of the novel, the clue to the eventual resolution of the plot when Wilson mentions the strawberry mark that would enable him to identify his lost son, although Joseph, whose true lineage is in the end revealed by this same birthmark, is sleeping on this occasion and does not hear him.

The epic structure of the novel is far less important to the historian of literature than the relationship the novel bears to *Pamela* and to *Shamela*. Fielding sets his story within the social framework of Richardson's masterpiece. Joseph is thought to be Pamela's brother; Lady Booby is the aunt of Mr. B--, in *Joseph Andrews* as in *Shamela* given the full name of Booby, and they are thus members of the same family created by Richardson. As the reader eventually learns, Joseph is really Mr. Wilson's son who had been stolen by gypsies, and Fanny, the girl left in his place, is the sister of Pamela.

The story of the novel is basically a simple one, in which Joseph's journey from London to Lady Booby's country seat forms the central portion of the action. A servant of Lady Booby and a physically attractive young man with a fine singing voice, Joseph accompanies his mistress to London, where he resists her amorous advances and, by so doing, provokes her anger to the point that he is dismissed from her service and forced to return home. On the way he meets Abraham Adams, his local parson, who accompanies him. On their journey home Joseph's chance rescue of his buxom and beautiful Fanny from an assault enables her to join him and the parson on the journey. After their return, their proposed nuptials are for a time interrupted by the news that they are in reality brother and sister, but this gloomy intelligence is dispelled by the discovery that Joseph is

Wilson's son, the strawberry mark on his breast serving as the infallible mark of his identity.

This brief outline of the central action gives nothing of the flavor or substance of the novel, which is filled with brilliantly contrived incidents that serve not merely to further the plot but to illustrate much of Fielding's conception of how the vanity and hypocrisy inherent in human life produce the ridiculous in man, the true source of comedy.

Fielding's sense of the pretentiousness of mankind leads to the gentle revelation of the foibles of the heroes and heroine of his story and to the slashing condemnation of the vicious hypocrisy of those who prey on their fellowmen with merciless success. Fielding returns to the objects of his attack in *Shamela,* thrusting again against Richardson's *Pamela,* Colley Cibber, and Conyers Middleton. He also examines directly the role of the parson and, most important, the relationship between human activity and charity. The wide disparity between reality and appearance is revealed on many levels of human activity, and what appears to be a rambling structure in the plotting of the novel takes on a thematic unity that is almost always apparent.

Joseph Andrews and *Shamela*

Fielding uses *Pamela* with considerable effect in developing his theme of the pretentious vanity of mankind. Not only does he retain the name and family connections of the heroine of Richardson's novel, but he sets Joseph and his actions with Lady Booby in comic contrast to the serious treatment in *Pamela* of the attempted seduction of the protagonist. Joseph's correspondence with his sister, as he believed her to be, maintains the fiction of Pamela's virtuous motives and her suitability as a model for the instruction of young women, much as Richardson had created it. But the publication of *Shamela* prior to *Joseph Andrews* should not be forgotten, for the true identity of Pamela as revealed in the spoof heightens the irony of her supposed ideal virtue in *Joseph Andrews.* Moreover, her social pretentiousness is emphasized strongly in her relationship with Fanny Goodwill before the latter is revealed to be her sister. Pamela corrects Joseph when he maintains that Fanny is her equal: "She was my equal," she responds, "but I am no longer Pamela Andrews; I am now this gentleman's lady, and, as such, am above her. I hope I shall never behave with an unbecoming pride: but, at the same time I shall always endeavour to know myself, and question not the assistance of grace to that purpose." She thus shares the sentiments of her husband, who would help Joseph to "make a figure in the world" if he does not "degrade" himself with his marriage to Fanny. *Joseph Andrews* moves well beyond being a parody of the sexual encounters of Richardson's novel and becomes a profound comment on the social customs of the day that separate classes not on the bases of substance and accomplishment but merely on those of wealth and birth. The arrogance of Mr. Booby and the dilemma faced by Joseph and Fanny are demonstrated in Booby's assertion to Joseph: "I must teach you the wide difference between us: my fortune enabled me to please myself; and it would have been as overgrown a folly in me to have omitted it as in you to do it" (bk. 4, chap. 7). The ironic force of Fielding's social viewpoint is driven home by the fact that Fanny is in reality Pamela's sister and must be accepted on equal terms by Mr. Booby in the end.

The introduction of Beau Didapper makes brilliant use of the attack on Conyers Middleton so effectively exploited in *Shamela*. Didapper, whose attempted assault on Fanny ironically punctuates the essential effeminacy of his character, is a thrust at Lord Hervey, ridiculed in the dedication of *Shamela* as Fanny, the name now applied to the perfection of country charm in Fielding's heroine. Hervey, it may be recalled, had been portrayed in Pope's *Epistle to Dr. Arbuthnot* as Sporus, "that mere white curd of Ass's milk."[7] Fielding's dislike of Middleton stemmed not only from his dedication of his *Life of Cicero* to Hervey, but also from his snide treatment, in its preface, of George Lyttleton's *Observations on the Life of Cicero*. Fielding had been a schoolmate of Lyttleton and seems to have had great admiration and respect for him as an individual as well as a member of the political opposition to Walpole. Beau Didapper, whose actions are as nakedly crude and offensive as those of any character in the novel, is advanced by Lady Booby as a lure to draw Fanny away from Joseph. In essence, the allurements of wealth, power, prestige, and the advantages of an elegant marriage are to be offered Fanny just as Leonora had been presented with similar temptations successfully in the first major digression of the novel. The echo of that digression emphasizes the most appealing aspect of Fanny's character, her complete and faithful loyalty to Joseph, just as the echo of the digressive story of Mr. Wilson, who succumbed in the early part of his career to the temptations of the town, stresses the moral strength of Joseph, who remains essentially innocent and unmoved by them.

The Clergy in *Joseph Andrews*

Fielding returns in *Joseph Andrews* to a theme he had introduced in *Shamela* and had treated extensively in the *Champion*—the proper conduct of the clergy and their necessary role in the social structure. In essays in the *Champion* on four successive Saturdays, beginning with that of Saturday, March 29, 1740, he offers his profile of what the clergy should be. He emphasizes that humility, charity, and poverty should characterize their lives and that they should be able to attend to their spiritual duties essentially free from temporal concerns. His concluding paper on the nineteenth of April condemns both deism and atheism.

Parson Adams is, of course, the chief vehicle in *Joseph Andrews* for expressing Fielding's ideas on the subject. In many respects he dominates the novel, especially in developing the intellectual basis of the book. Although Adams is a comic figure, his eccentricities serve to emphasize those qualities that Fielding found most essential to the clergy—humility and charity. His life illustrates the view that poverty is an ideal, at least in the sense that the clergy should accumulate no fortune, vast or modest, at the expense of their spiritual obligations. He is comically bookish and absentminded, his experience with life often drawn solely from that select classical reading with which he is acquainted. His lack of worldly experience seems to make him unaware of the viciousness of others, and a ready victim of their cruel humor. In reality, Adams is victimized not so much by his lack of awareness, as by his giving the benefit of the doubt to others. He offers the open hand of friendship, and, if it is accepted, as it often is, he acts with the charitable humility proper to his role as a parson. When it is rejected, he reacts with an exaggerated dignity and excusable vanity. In the eyes of the worldly pragmatist he is a comic figure and the butt of malicious humor. But such vulnerability is inevitable for the man of the cloth who cannot accept cynical protective devices that might shield him from insult.

The role of the clergyman is inevitably foolish by materialistic standards, but not by those manifested in charity and humility. On their journey home Adams and his companions are attacked by the hounds of a group of hunters who sense that Adams might be an entertaining victim of their practical jokes. The local squire, who is among the hunters, invites Adams to his estate. Educated at home, their host had devoted most of his life to hunting and similar pleasures of the country. He had traveled through Europe for three years, absorbing all the extravagances of the Continent and had surrounded himself with companions of an odd and eccentric sort, "gentlemen of cur-like disposition who were now at his house, and whom he had brought with him from London." They were, Fielding tells us, "an old half-pay officer, a player, a dull poet, a quack doctor, a scraping fiddler, and a lame German dancing-master." This assortment of misfits proceeds to abuse Adams. The sport is punctuated by

Adams's pompous speech criticizing their assault on him as a clergyman, and by his amiably vain assertion that he is not in need of charity, producing, as proof, his one half-guinea, not "out of ostentation of riches" but merely to convince them he speaks the truth. Adams thus evokes a mock apology from the doctor, which he accepts with true Christian humility, declaring that everything is forgiven. But the fun of the evening continues, as Adams is encouraged to give a sermon and tricked into falling into a tub of water (bk. 3, chap. 7).

The incident serves well to characterize Adams, who acts with admirable restraint in the face of insult to himself. On other occasions, where an individual is known or suspected to be in distress, he invariably rushes to the person's defense and applies what physical measures are needed to secure his safety. However impetuous he is in defense of others, he is slow to take offense and ready to measure out forgiveness where he himself is involved. It is not that he is unaware of what is happening but that through an habitual and conscious effort his initial reaction to others is marked with a charity that can be abused.

Adams is not merely a model of charity, but a man who preaches and performs necessary religious duties called for by his position. His view of religion is punctuated by his desire to have Joseph and Fanny married with the approved religious ceremony, rather than by license. And when the marriage takes place, he finds it necessary to rebuke Pamela and Mr. Booby for laughing "in so sacred a place, and on so solemn an occasion." In matters of religion Adams tends to be without humor. "It was his maxim," Fielding observes, "that he was a servant of the Highest, and could not, without departing from his duty, give up the least article of his honour or of his cause to the greatest earthly potentate. Indeed, he always asserted that Mr. Adams at church with his surplice on, and Mr. Adams without that ornament in any other place, were two very different persons" (bk. 4, chap. 16).

In addition to Adams other parsons are introduced in the novel and illustrate how the clergy should act. The serious devotion of the clergy to their role involved avoiding an unnecessary concern for material things. Among the laws approved by Fielding in the *Champion* was that dealing with the ownership of land: "Nay, so careful is the law, that the clergy should not be any ways hindered or disturbed in their spiritual office, that they are forbid to take any lands to farm or to buy and sell in markets, &c., under very severe penalties, that nothing might prevent them from discharging their duties to the souls of men" (April 12, 1740). The violation of at least the spirit of this law is personified in the character of Parson Trulliber, whom Adams encounters on his journey.

Parson Trulliber is the antithesis of Adams. While Adams devotes his life entirely to his vocation, Trulliber is a parson on Sunday, a farmer on the other days of the week. Unable to pay for the charges of his party at the local inn, Adams remembers that there is a neighboring clergyman and applies to him for a loan, expecting a generous response to his request, but he finds Trulliber a difficult person to approach. Not that he is not well received when he approaches Trulliber's door, but he is welcome only because he is mistaken for a dealer who has come to purchase the farmer's hogs. When Trulliber learns of Adams's true mission, he quickly and rudely refuses him. All of this leads to a debate between the two parsons on the true nature of Christianity, and finally reverts to one of the important themes Fielding had introduced in *Shamela,* the relationship that exists between faith and good works.

"I would have thee punished as a vagabond for thy impudence," Trulliber declares. "Fourteen shillings indeed! I won't give thee a farthing. I believe thou art no more a clergyman than the woman there (pointing to his wife); but if thou art, dost deserve to have thy gown stript over thy shoulders for running about the country in such a manner." The argument that ensues centers initially on charity and finally faith and good works: "I am sorry," answered Adams, "that you do know what charity is, since you practise it no better; I must tell you, if you trust to your knowledge for justification, you will find yourself deceived, though you should add faith to it, without good works" (bk. 2, chap. 14). In having Trulliber reject what Fielding sees to be the central duty of the Christian, a charitable relationship to his fellowman, he adds a new dimension to the portrayal of the worldly clergyman that he had previously created in Parson Williams in *Shamela.* The vice is different, but the worldly orientation of the two men leads to a view of Christianity that asserts a belief in religion, while neglecting those things implicit in such belief. The worldly clergyman thus becomes the supreme example of the hypocrisy of vice parading as virtue.

Charity in *Joseph Andrews*

Fielding sets a high standard for the clergy, but the demands of charity extend as well to others who pose as Christians. Charity among the citizenry at large is studied by Fielding through a series of visits which Adams and Joseph make to inns and alehouses, as they pursue their journey. At the first major inn in which Joseph stops, that of the Sign of the Dragon conducted by Mr. and Mrs. Tow-wouse, he is joined by Parson Adams. At this public gathering place, Fielding finds opportunity to develop an extensive pattern of comment on charity through the actions of a variety of people of different types and occupations.

Fielding prepares for the treatment of the theme of charity at the Sign of the Dragon by the adventures Joseph encounters before reaching it. After setting out for London alone and on foot, he is forced to seek shelter from a storm at an inn conducted by a friendly and amiable individual who recognizes him as a servant of Mr. Booby by his livery. Here Joseph meets a neighboring servant whom he accompanies to a second inn, where he remains only briefly before setting out again on foot. On this part of the journey he is attacked, beaten, robbed, and left naked in a ditch by the side of the road. A passing stagecoach stops when the postilion hears him groan. The reactions of the passengers of the coach reveal in varying degrees their collectively callous attitude toward the man in trouble. A genteel lady is disturbed at his nakedness; an old gentleman would leave in haste for fear that they will be the last to see him if he should die, a circumstance that might cause them legal difficulties. A lawyer finally prevails on the group to bring Joseph to an inn to save his life, for fear that if he should die they might be accused of murder. The lady refuses to admit Joseph into the coach naked, and Joseph himself, following the example, as he tells us, of "the amiable Pamela, and the excellent sermons of Mr. Adams," refuses to enter the coach unclothed. No one will spare a coat until the postilion, a young man who had been transported for robbing a henroost, offers his, and the coach is able to proceed to the next inn (bk. 1, chap. 12).

At the Sign of the Dragon, Joseph is well enough received initially. Betty, the maid, is prepared to find him a bed, and Mr. Tow-wouse sends her for one of his shirts. But the reaction of Mrs. Two-wouse is another matter. Fielding's physical description of her reinforces the distortion of her character:

Her person was short, thin, and crooked. Her forehead projected in the middle, and thence descended in a declivity to the top of her nose, which was sharp and red, and would have hung over her lips, had not nature turned up the end of it. Her lips were two bits of skin, which, whenever she spoke, she drew together in a purse. Her chin was peaked, and at the upper end of that skin which composed her cheeks stood two bones, that almost hid a pair of small red eyes. Add to this a voice most wonderfully adapted to the sentiments it was to convey, being both loud and hoarse. (bk. 1, chap. 14).

The creature thus portrayed becomes early in the book a spokesman for the purely pragmatic, unsympathetic, and uncharitable view of life that arises again and again in the novel. Here, her termagant nature is balanced by the milder and more charitable instincts of her husband, and by the kindness of their maid, Betty.

The contrasting attitudes of husband and wife are demonstrated dramatically in chapter 12 of the first book of the novel. The argument is over the shirt that Mr. Tow-wouse has sent Betty to procure in order to clothe the destitute Joseph. Mrs. Tow-wouse shouts: "What the devil do you mean by this, Mr. Tow-wouse? Am I to buy shirts to lend to a set of scabby rascals?" "My dear," said Mr. Tow-wouse, "this is a poor wretch." "Yes," says she, "I know it is a poor wretch; but what the devil have we to do with poor wretches? The law makes us provide for too many already. We shall have thirty or forty poor wretches in red coats shortly." "My dear," cries Tow-wouse, "this man hath been robbed of all he hath." "Well then," said she, "where's his money to pay his reckoning? Why doth not such a fellow go to an alehouse? I shall send him packing as soon as I am up, I assure you." "My dear," said he, "common charity won't suffer you to do that" "Common charity, a f—t!" says she, "common charity teaches us to provide for ourselves and our families; and I and mine won't be ruined by your charity, I assure you." "Well," says he, "my dear, do as you will when you are up; you know I never contradict you." "No," says she; "if the devil was to contradict me, I would make the house too hot to hold him."

This scene demonstrates Fielding's ability to handle dialogue and to create incidents illustrative of the social views he is attempting to clarify. The physical description of Mrs. Tow-wouse, which the novelist withholds until well into the next chapter, serves to reinforce the meaning of the scene. Her nature and her attitudes are embodied in her physical appearance. As Fielding himself puts it ". . . if Mrs. Tow-wouse had given no utterance to the sweetness of her temper, nature had taken such pains in her countenance, that Hogarth himself never gave more expression to a picture" (bk. 1, chap. 14).

The trio of characters who conduct the business at the inn serve to illustrate in a lesser way a key moral question developed more centrally in Fielding's later novels, *Tom Jones* and *Amelia,* where both heroes, Tom and Captain Booth, pay little attention to the moral aspect of their sexual activities throughout much of those tales. Tom Jones engages in three major sexual encounters, with Molly Straddle, with Mrs. Waters, and with Lady Bellaston, before marrying Sophia; and Captain Booth, while married to Amelia, engages in an adulterous relationship with Miss Matthews while they share a prison cell. Obviously, Fielding is not attempting to suggest that no moral standards exist, nor is he approving of these activities by Tom and Booth. But he does take advantage of the wide condemnation of such activities by individuals who lack rudimentary charitable instincts, to demonstrate the distorted perspective of their social attitudes. For Fielding, charity or the willingness to assist another in need is a far greater virtue than chastity, and the uncharitable individual is far more to be condemned than Tom Jones or Captain Booth who, through human weakness, fall into a vice that is not reflective of ill nature and that does no immediate or positive harm to a fellow human being. This relationship between sex and charity is introduced in the Tow-wouse episode by having Betty, the charitable maid, and Mr. Tow-wouse, the charitable innkeeper, take advantage of the momentary absence of Mrs. Tow-wouse to indulge their mutual passion, she having just been rejected by the virtuous Joseph and he worn down by the termagant verbal assaults of his wife. Unfortunately for both, Mrs. Tow-wouse discovers them just accomplishing the deed. Betty is discharged, and Mr. Tow-wouse condemned to a lifetime of wifely recrimination. Mrs. Tow-wouse is not condemned by society for her lack of charity, but she is able to turn society's often-hypocritical attitudes toward sex to her advantage.

The adventures at the Dragon also introduce Mr. Barnabas, a parson of little true love for his fellowman, but of admirable theological conviction. Unlike Trulliber, who appears later in the novel, he is an amiable and sociable individual when not called upon for devotion to religious exercises. His leisurely attitude toward his calling is demonstrated by the manner in which he responds to the call for a minister when Joseph is brought into the inn and believed to be dying. "Mr. Barnabas . . . came as soon as sent for; and, having first drank a dish of tea with the landlady, and afterwards a bowl of punch with the landlord, he walked up to the room where Joseph lay; . . ." (bk. 1, chap. 13). Later on, he engages with Parson Adams in a theological discourse that evolves out of the discussion of the possibility of publishing Adams's sermons, when a bookseller who is present declares that he "would as soon print one of Whitefield's as any farce whatever" (bk. 1, chap. 17).

The bookseller's suggestion leads Barnabas to a condemnation of Whitefield, but in terms that reveal his own flaccid view of his vocation: "Sir," said he, turning to Adams, "this fellow's writings (I know not whether you have seen them) are levelled at the clergy. He would reduce us to the example of the primitive ages, forsooth! and would insinuate to the people that a clergyman ought to be always preaching and praying. He pretends to understand the Scripture literally; and would make mankind believe that the poverty and low estate which was recommended to the church in its infancy, and was only temporary doctrine adapted to her under persecution, was to be preserved in her flourishing and established state. Sir, the principles of Toland, Woolston, and all the free-thinkers, are not calculated to do half the mischief, as those professed by this fellow and his followers" (bk. 1, chap. 17). Fielding, through the device of having Barnabas condemn the Methodists, reveals those tendencies among the clergy of his day that he feels are to be condemned: their worldliness, their lack of attention to prayer, their individual interpretation of Scripture, and, most of all, their flirting with and hospitality toward freethinking and atheism.

The condemnation of Methodism by Fielding elsewhere in his works is not contradicted by this passage, for what Barnabas criticizes in Whitefield and his followers are those aspects of their teaching that are essentially traditional and therefore not attacked by Fielding. Their assertion of the primacy of the religious function of the clergy is precisely what irritates Barnabas, but is defended by Parson Adams. Adams, thus, responds by lending support to Whitefield's objection to the amassing of luxury by the clergy. This does not prevent Adams's condemning Whitefield's evangelical excesses and the Methodist's blurring of the relationship between belief and conduct. Echoing one of the important themes advanced by Fielding both in the periodicals and in *Shamela,* Adams declares: ". . . when he began to call nonsense and enthusiasm to his aid, and set up the detestable doctrine of faith against good works, I was his friend no longer; for surely that doctrine was coined in hell . . ." (bk. 1, chap. 12). The argument between the bookseller and Barnabas on the one hand and Adams on the other picks up intensity until it is finally interrupted by the thunderous excitement caused by Mrs. Tow-wouse's discovery of her husband and Betty in bed.

Adams and Joseph continue their journey, meeting both the good and the bad of the English citizenry. When they reach the inn of Boniface, the roles of husband and wife are the reverse of what they had been at the Dragon, the wife ready to extend the hand of charity and the husband more materially concerned with pleasing only those guests who can pay well. At this inn one of the brilliantly comic fights in which Parson Adams engages takes place when the patient clergyman is sparked to physical action by the surly disposition of the host. In ludicrous fashion the scene imitates the battle scenes of the serious epic. The incident grows out of the host's objection to the charitable treatment of Joseph, who has been wounded, this time by having been thrown from Adams's capricious horse. Joseph angers the host by referring to Adams as his "better," and as Boniface directs him out of his house and approaches him, as though to physically accomplish that objective, Adams rushes to his friend's defense. The exchange of blows that follows finds the host stretched on the floor, at which sight the lady of the house rushes to her husband's aid, pouring a basin of hog's blood over the head of Adams. Matters are finally put to rights and the journey continues, Joseph agreeing to join the ladies in the coach, Adams to continue on horseback.

The absentmindedness of Adams leads to another heroic battle. On this occasion, without knowing her identity, he rescues a young woman who is assaulted by a fellow traveler on her way to London. Adams, forgetting that he had his horse with him, had set out on foot in full stride and, outstripping the stagecoach, found himself off the beaten track. There he met a stranger, and while they were conversing, heard a girl scream and, neglecting the advice of his companion, rushed to her defense. Fielding details the story, using in comic fashion all the devices with which tales of combat are related in the serious epic, including the heroic simile. As Adams approaches his adversary, who has the young woman firmly in hand, the novelist describes the action: "As the game cock, when engaged in amorous toying with a hen, if perchance he espies another cock at hand, immediately quits his female, and opposes himself to his rival, so did the ravisher, on the information of the crabstick, immediately leap from the woman, and hasten to assail the man" (bk. 2, chap. 9). The battle is fiercely fought with Adams emerging the victor. Fielding uses the mock-epic battle here, not merely to advance the story, but to add detail and dimension to his portrait of Adams both as clergyman and human being. He is a more complex character than might at first appear, and his readiness for battle in instances where the innocent are in distress offsets the quiet patience he habitually practices.

Characterization in *Joseph Andrews*

Of the major characters in the novel, Parson Adams is the most strikingly portrayed. His physical attributes admirably complement those characteristics of personality and moral stature that form his character. Fielding, as narrator, tells the reader that he was well acquainted with both Adams and Joseph and that they are the sources of the information in the novel. Fielding allows the details of Adams's appearance to emerge slowly, and there is a cumulative buildup of factors that accentuate the parson's eccentricities. He is extremely tall, thin, and athletic. He is proud of his physical strength, and he successfully challenges a stagecoach to test its speed against his walking ability. His mannerism of snapping his fingers when excited, his constant reading of Aeschylus, and his forgetfulness induced by a lack of concentration on worldly things contribute to the general physical picture of him that emerges. Before he reaches the end of his journey, his adventures have served to alter his appearance and to intensify its oddity. He starts out wearing a short, white greatcoat with black buttons, and a somewhat torn cassock tucked up under it. Three major incidents change the whiteness of his garment: he is covered with hog's blood at the inn of Mr. Boniface; he falls in the slop of Trulliber's pigs; and he is finally doused in a tub of water by the unruly companions of the country squire. The comic potential of visualizing all this should not be forgotten as he travels across the countryside and is treated with varying degrees of respect. In an age where clothing is a mark of rank, Adams becomes an increasingly curious and strange figure.

More puzzling and in need of examination than Adams's appearance is what he does. A man of true humility, he appears proud because of the way he asserts himself in argument. He manifests the assurance of the narrowly learned man, whose experience with books is his substitute for experience in life. Fielding is not suggesting that the experience of books is necessarily bad, nor that it is not in some respects more valid than the essentially narrow life experiences the ordinary individual has. But Adams's bookish view of life is incomprehensible to those whose experience is essentially that of the real world. The classical orientation of his life is punctuated by his Aeschylus, a hand-copied volume of the Greek dramatist's work. His admiration for the Greek playwright does not broaden his respect for the contemporary theater, which he condemns as immoral, although he has read only one modern tragedy, Addison's *Cato*. When he attempts to converse with Barnabas or Trulliber, it is apparent that he does not speak their language, for their understanding has been little shaped by study, but, in large measure, by the concerns of everyday existence and the pursuit of material success. Adams finds his way through life, oblivious of material concerns. Money means nothing to him, position is irrelevant, and only a desire to help his fellowman is of vital concern. For this reason, his minor vanities, his love of the classics, his pride in physical achievements, his admiration of the accomplishments of his children, and his insistence on the dignity of his office become amiable eccentricities that add to, rather than detract from, the attractiveness of his character.

Joseph obviously admires Adams but his admiration is carefully adjusted by common sense. Joseph is no naive lad, prudishly defying the ability of Mrs. Booby to seduce him early in the book. He is as aware of life as any young man his age could be, but his awareness is on the side of the angels. Although it is a year since he has seen his beloved Fanny, he has a heart only for her. A favorite among the footmen of London, he accompanies them in their normal diversions. His beautiful voice gives him an interest in singing that makes him a minor expert on opera and something of an authority among his fellows. He is good-looking, tall, beautifully built physically, and possessed of magnificent hair which he carefully grooms in the best manner of London servants. Joseph has been an apprentice with the Boobys since he was ten years old, and his interests are largely male-oriented; he loves hunting and horses and performs all allied activities with admirable skill. He is not unmindful of the ladies, but his amorous inclinations are fixed on the buxom Fanny, and it is perhaps the memory of her as much as the instruction of Adams that keeps him from being tempted by Lady Booby, Slipslop, or even the servant, Betty.

Fielding uses Adams and Joseph to reinforce the characterization of each other. Each possesses a goodness and charity that emerge differently in individuals who are strikingly diverse in age, temperament, and experience; and each finds his idealism challenged by the realities of existence. Adams's intellectual inflexibility is hardly suited to his more emotion-driven humanity in moments of great personal crisis. Fielding demonstrates this for the reader by having Adams discuss with Joseph the control of his passions. The dialogue is interrupted by word that the parson's son has drowned, and he falls into an immoderate expression of grief. No sooner does news of his child's rescue come than he continues to lecture Joseph on moderation. Joseph, driven to the limit of his patience, expostulates that it is "easier to give advice than to take it," and that Adams did not "so entirely conquer himself, when he apprehended he had lost his son, or when he found him recovered" (bk. 4, chap. 8). Adams weakly defends himself, noting that only a father can understand fatherly love. Moreover, he rejects Joseph's suggestion that his love for Fanny is as great as the parson's for his son, and he asserts that husbands should love their wives with "moderation and discretion," thus intellectually belying the truly great and immoderate love he himself has demonstrated for his wife.

Fielding's portrayal of Adams reveals his humanity without destroying the essential model of charity that he is. Adams's bookish sense of the world yields to his experiential sense of what is right. What he does reveals more than what he says in the incident regarding his son's supposed drowning. Such incidents are essential to the novel and to the characterization of Adams, for despite his withdrawal from the things of the world, he lives in it, and, particularly in his relationships with his immediate family and friends, there is the necessary application of his ideals to the immediacy of daily experience. Although his words may sound foolish when reduced to the naked statement of argument, his actions counter their effect. Adams's sense of charity and virtue, intellectually grounded as it is, is acted out in the experience of day-to-day existence. What he does is more an index of the man than what he says since he acts by an almost instinctive sense that is the result of the habitual practice of charity.

A more passively drawn character than Adams, Joseph still has spirit when he needs to call on it, and his reaction to Adams's insistence on his moderation in love shows a fire that even his extreme respect for the parson cannot withstand. From a sentimental point of view, his loyal and determined affection for Fanny is his strongest virtue.

Fanny appears late in the novel and is not sharply characterized. Of all the characters in the novel she is, perhaps, the least aware of the world and her accepting a stranger's invitation to allow him to accompany her on her journey to London seems incredibly naive. While it is obvious that Fielding needs some set of circumstances to unite her with Adams and Joseph on their trip home, Fielding capitalizes on the scene to emphasize Fanny's retiring nature. After she is rescued by Adams, she does in fact begin to fear him, but she does not attempt to run and mildly places herself in his hands. Fanny is more comfortable dissolved in tears than in asserting her prerogatives when in trouble, and the initial description of her given by Fielding emphasizes her bashfulness, a not unattractive feature that is balanced by exquisite sensibility and sweetness. The physical description of Fanny introduces touches of imperfection that serve to enhance her beauty, rather than diminish it, for they sound a realistic note that adds to its credibility. Fanny's teeth, for example, are not exactly even; her arms are a little reddened by her labor; and the smallpox has left a single mark on her chin. But the overall picture of her is one of a delightfully natural and well-endowed country girl:

Fanny was now in the nineteenth year of her age; she was tall and delicately shaped, but not one of those slender young women who seem rather intended to hang up in the hall of an anatomist than for any other purpose. On the contrary, she was so plump that she seemed bursting through her tight stays, especially in the part which confined her swelling breasts. Nor did her hips want the assistance of a hoop to extend them. . . . Her complexion was fair, a little injured by the sun, but overspread with such a bloom that the finest ladies would have exchanged all their white for it: add to these a countenance in which, though she was extremely bashful, a sensibility appeared almost incredible; and a sweetness, whenever she smiled, beyond either imitation or description. To conclude all, she had a natural gentility, superior to the acquisition of art, and which surprised all who beheld her. (bk. 2, chap. 12).

In the final analysis she is a wonderful complement to Joseph, for together they possess the charming ebullience of natural spirit that accepts the reality of sex without the suggestion of the lustful extravagance of Slipslop and Lady Booby, who appear in marked contrast to her. In his characterization of Joseph and Fanny, Fielding portrays a love that in them is not prudish but natural and that exudes attractive innocence rather than artificial pretense and hypocrisy.

The lesser characters of Lady Booby and Slipslop are effective comic portraits, bordering on caricature, but not sufficiently exaggerated to remove them from recognizable humanity. Slipslop seems to be the first major effort in English literature to employ malapropisms and distortions of words as means of characterizing a female character. The misuse of language by Slipslop emphasizes her attempt to maintain a level of dignity based on learning that derives from the fact that she is the daughter of a clergyman. Not well educated, she has sufficient familiarity with difficult words to prompt her to use them, although frequently in the wrong way. Her pretensions to learning are further indicated by her frequent disputes with Adams on theological matters. Fielding smiles at the desire of uneducated individuals to participate in the discussion of matters that are often beyond their knowledge and experience. He ridicules the tendency of a broad range of society to engage in such discussion in his papers on the Robinhood Society in the *Covent Garden Journal*.[8] Here, though the satire is more particularized, it thrusts generally in the same direction.

Slipslop, at the age of forty-five, feels that life has passed her by, at least in matters of love, and, although she had made a single "slip" in her youth, she has maintained her chastity ever since. Because she has passed the age of childbearing and feels no danger in that regard, she casts desirous eyes on Joseph and, in this respect, becomes the rival of her mistress, Lady Booby. This juxtaposition of two older women in rivalry for the love of a reluctant young servant is an excellent comic device. Mrs. Booby, having recently been widowed by Sir Thomas, finds her footman, Joseph, irresistible and her attempts to seduce him are clear echoes of her nephew's attempt to seduce Pamela in Richardson's novel. But Fielding has more at stake than a mere parody of *Pamela*. The interrelationship of Slipslop and Lady Booby in their lust for Joseph continues throughout the novel and is responsible for much hilarity as the novel comes to its end.

Lady Booby's interest in Joseph began even before the death of her husband. Although it resulted only in her walking arm in arm with him on appropriate occasions, it was enough to evoke comment from Lady Tittle and Lady Tattle. These innocent freedoms, however, are insufficient for the lady once Sir Thomas Booby dies. After a period of mourning, lasting one week and mostly taken up with playing cards with Slipslop and three women friends, she alters her approach to Joseph. When her advances are ignored and she dismisses her footman in a fit of pique, the main action of the novel is set in motion. Lady Booby appears little during the central portion of the novel, but Slipslop, the more pleasant of the two toward the world at large, appears at appropriate times throughout. After all have reached their destination in the country, Lady Booby again emerges, and her jealous and malevolent rage is turned to the task of separating Joseph and Fanny and of frustrating their marriage. Always an unattractive personality, Lady Booby emerges in increasingly dark colors as she adds Fanny to Joseph as a target of her malevolence and obscene jealousy.

Plot and Structure

Much has been said about the weaknesses of the plot structure of *Joseph Andrews*. Chance occurrences can be viewed as needed to move a faltering plot in the right direction. Digressions can be pointed to as distracting the reader from the main thrust of the story. Characters may seem to be improbable and overly exaggerated, and Adams and Joseph too sentimentally oriented toward religion, on the one hand, and romantic love on the other. These supposed weaknesses may be viewed as strengths if we look at *Joseph Andrews*, not in terms of the conventional plot, character, and theme analysis that might be applied to the traditional novel, but as an experimental art form designed to project Fielding's insight into reality. From this point of view, the exaggerations of character and the idiosyncrasies of plot may be seen as part of a well-designed structure. When, in the opening chapter, Fielding ironically cites Pamela Andrews and her history as an example of the apt portrayal of virtue for the efficacious example of the reader, he is counting on the knowledge of his own *Shamela* to make clear his meaning, just as his prior ridicule of Colley Cibber, both in the *Champion* and *Shamela,* functions in the same manner. What Fielding has done is to set up a world of fiction created by the two previous works, *Pamela* and *Shamela,* into which he can introduce characters that move comfortably. The identity of Pamela is retained in *Shamela,* Fielding's spoof of Richardson's novel, by the simple device of allowing the heroine to possess two identities, that of Pamela by which she is known to Mr. B--, and that of Shamela by which she is known to Parson Oliver. The novel and the spoof are not mutually contradictory, they simply reveal the duplicity of Pamela, her parents, and Parson Williams, a duplicity that completely fools Mr. Booby. In what might be considered the sequel to *Pamela* and *Shamela,* since it follows them in time, *Joseph Andrews* continues to present Pamela and her husband in the terms created by Richardson.

All of the characters of *Joseph Andrews* who appear in the main action of the story are distortions of reality as the ordinary reader would perceive the world—but not distorted, if seen from the perspective of the novelist as he senses the disparity between appearance and reality and strives to create an artistic vehicle to convey his perceptions. Thus Lady Booby, who might appear to the world as a pompous and dictatorial woman with merely formal affection for her late husband, in the novel becomes a sexually aggressive female, prepared to take advantage of his death to bring to fruition the lust for Joseph which she had felt even before her husband's death. She is careful to create a reason for Joseph's dismissal, his supposed amorous interference with the morals of the other servants, whom she would appear to the world to be protecting. But in the world of fiction in which Fielding exposes the hypocritical nature of things, the tawdriness of her motives revealed here in the early part of the novel supports the viciousness of her actions toward Joseph and Fanny in the later portions of the book.

Similarly, to the eye of the ordinary observer of life, the idyllic love of Fanny and Joseph may seem excessively dipped in sentimental honey. But when, stripped of all pretense, it is recognized as representative of true and abiding love and allowed to emerge as emblematic of the lack of concern of young and true love for all outside itself, it fits admirably within the created world of the novel. Adams himself is less an eccentric than the personification of the total commitment of the clergy to religion and virtue. The unworldly orientation of Adams's approach to life appropriately lacks sham and pretense. Fielding, in order to unmask pretension to virtue and to reveal the deceitful nature of vice, has created a fictitious world to which eccentricity of character and unpredictability of action are essential.

The world Fielding creates is a ridiculous world, but in creating a new genre, the comic epic in prose, designed to deal with the ridiculous, he makes such a world inevitable. In this sense it is admirably consistent from the amiable affectations of Adams, to the exaggerated sentimentalism of Joseph and Fanny, to the malevolence of Lady Booby, and to the revolting effeminacy of Beau Didapper. In the digressive tales the world is appropriately less distorted. Leonora acts toward Bellarmine in a manner expected by the world at large, and she reaps the predictable disappointments; Mr. Wilson moves into the world in a realistic and inexperienced manner, and only bitter experience shows him the proper way to go. But Fielding's world, with its inhabitants opened to us in a manner that strips them of their asserted motives and reveals them through the prism of the ridiculous, takes on a truth and realism of its own. This realism bursts the bounds of convention and produces scenes that are truly funny and productive of laughter, but also truly comic in demonstrating the ultimate limits of pretense.

The brilliantly comic bedroom episode in chapter 14 of the last book is a case in point, and it is one of the most hilarious actions in the novel. Its laughter punctuates the serious theme of the hypocrisy and pretense of life in a manner that only the laughter of ridicule can. Beau Didapper, the effeminate figure of Lord Hervey, unmindful of the chaste virtue of Joseph and Fanny, decides to impersonate Joseph and sleep with Fanny. It is a ludicrous concept to the reader, but to the vain conceit of Didapper, who can make no distinction between his own effeminacy and Joseph's virility, his ability to fool Fanny by mimicking Joseph's voice offers no problem. When he finds Slipslop, rather than Fanny, in the bed, the scene erupts as she, wishing to bolster a flagging reputation for chaste virtue, holds fast to the beau and screams for help. A rapid change takes place as Adams, always ready to leap to the defense of innocence in distress, rushes from his own bed, clad only in a nightcap, and seeks to effect a rescue. In the darkness he understandably mistakes Didapper for the woman in the case and proceeds to subdue Slipslop, enabling Didapper to effect his escape. Lady Booby, having heard the commotion, enters as Slipslop continues to cry rape, and mistakes what has happened. Adams's position, naked in Slipslop's bed, makes him the apparent rapist: "She then began to revile the parson as the wickedest of all men, and particularly railed at his impudence in choosing her house for the scene of his debaucheries, and her own woman for the object of his bestiality." Fortunately for Adams, Didapper, in disrobing, had left portions of his unmistakably ornate clothing in the room, and the hilarity of the scene reaches a crescendo as this truth is brought to light. But Fielding has more in store for his reader, as the world of the ridiculous makes the improbable possible, and before

morning Adams is once more to mistake himself, only to find himself in
Fanny's bed as Joseph comes to greet her at dawn. Fielding has sought out
the most improbable of situations and has succeeded by a brilliant se-
quence of incidents to bring it about. Such incidents, moreover, focus
attention on the theme of the conflict between appearance and reality,
demonstrating that appearances often distort the ability to recognize
reality, and that men possess a profound capacity for placing on extraneous
sources the blame for their mistakes, however innocent. Even after discov-
ering that he found himself in Fanny's bed because he had absentmindedly
confused left and right, Adams continues to mutter to himself that the
power of witchcraft could not be denied by a Christian. Despite overwhelming evidence, the reality of his mistake is not entirely accepted by
the parson.

A Journey from this World to the Next

A Journey from this World to the Next is an extremely free exploitation of
Lucian's *Dialogues of the Dead,* in which Fielding imaginatively explores his
ideas on charity, human pretense, and the materialistic thrust of society, in
a format that lies between the expository prose of the periodical and the
artistic requirements of the novel. Fielding had used Lucian's *Dialogues of
the Dead* previously in the puppet show portion of *The Author's Farce,* in the
unsuccessful play *Eurydice,* in the short unstaged dramatic work, *A
Dialogue between Alexander the Great and Diogenes the Cynic,* as well as in the
"Vision of Charon's Boat" in the *Champion* of May 24, 1740. But none of
these efforts possess the imaginative quality and ambitious scope of the
Journey.

The work purports to be the autobiographical account of the narrator's
adventures from the time his soul leaves his body after death until it finds
its way to happiness in the afterlife. Fielding's narrator emphasizes the
sense of liberty and freedom felt by the soul separated from the flesh: "No
prisoner discharged from a long confinement, ever tasted the sweets of
liberty with a more exquisite relish, than I enjoyed in this delivery from a
dungeon wherein I had been detained upwards of forty years, . . ." (bk. 1,
chap. 1). He soon meets a gentleman in a silk waistcoat who informs him
that since he has died a natural death he must set out immediately for the
other world. Mercury, whom he shortly encounters, directs him to the
spot where he boards the stagecoach to the underworld with six fellow
passengers. Their journey takes them to the City of Diseases, the Palace of
Death, and finally to the River Cocytus, which, leaving their coach

behind, they cross by boat. On the other side they meet a number of other spirits who move in the opposite direction, returning to the flesh at a point where the roads to Greatness and to Goodness meet. Although the road to Goodness is more pleasant than the hard and craggy route to Greatness, all but a very few souls choose that to Greatness because on that route they are greeted by "the music of drums and trumpets, and the perpetual acclamations of the mob" (bk. 1, chap. 5). He views the Wheel of Fortune by which the fate of those who are to enter the world is decided. Each occupation or station in life to which a person might be called is balanced by other life factors that tend to equalize the various choices. For example, the lot of the cobbler is accompanied by sickness and good humor, that of the general, by honor and discontent. In addition, each person is destined for the celibate or the married life, the latter "being all marked with a large pair of horns" (bk. 1, chap. 6).

At the gates of Elysium to which they finally arrive, the porter, Minos, subjects each soul to an examination, those only being admitted who have done some positive good in their lives and possess charity. The alternatives to entering Elysium are to be thrown into the bottomless pit for those who are totally reprobate, or to be sent back into the world to be further purged of vice for those who have demonstrated some redeeming feature in the life they have led on earth. Pertinent examples of different types of men, which reveal clearly the difference between worldly and other-worldly realities, parade to Minos for judgment, and most are sent back to the world to try again. The story of the narrator himself provides a good summary of the life values that are explored in Fielding's other works, both fictitious and nonfictitious. He approaches his judge with diffidence: "I confessed I had indulged myself very freely with wine and women in my youth, but had never done an injury to any man living, nor avoided an opportunity of doing good, that I pretended to very little virtue more than general philanthropy and private friendship" (bk. 5, chap. 7). Unexpectedly, he is moved forward by Minos. The narrator has traits of character found in Tom Jones, but not in the heroes of Fielding's two previous novels, *Joseph Andrews* and *Jonathan Wild*. Like Tom, Joseph, and Heartfree, he is a man of good will and fundamental charity, but like Tom alone, he is guilty, at least in youth, of sexual excess.

Once crossed to Elysium, the narrator encounters the great literary figures who have passed on, both ancient and of more recent date. He also meets other famous personages, such as the actors, Betterton and Booth, and, surprisingly, Oliver Cromwell, who, on a return to earth has purged his earlier life by a distressful existence as a soldier wounded in the Battle of the Boyne and reduced to extreme poverty by supporting a wife and seven children. Finally, the narrator comes upon Julian the Apostate, whose story takes up the next major portion of the work. He is amazed at finding Julian, who he feels deserved the bottomless pit as much as any man. As he relates his story, Julian maintains that many untruths have been spread about him, and that he was forced to return to earth many times to purge himself of the evil lives he led. Finally, his martyrdom as Archbishop Hugh Latimer achieved his salvation. His various transmigrations have taken him into many different characters including those of a slave, a Jew, a general, a carpenter, a beau, a monk, a king, a fool, and a statesman. The manuscript breaks off before Julian completes his story, but we learn that he returned as a bishop three times before his final martyrdom. From a note at the end of book 1, itself incomplete, we learn that the manuscript contains nothing more until chapter 7 of book 19, the story of Anna Boleyn, written in a different handwriting from the rest and told by the lady herself. The *Journey* ends with her story, the rest of the manuscript having been "destroyed in rolling up pens, tobacco, etc" (Final Note).

A Journey from this World to the Next is one of the least appreciated works of Fielding in relation to its actual achievement. From a literary point of view, it has clearly less importance than *Joseph Andrews* or even *Jonathan Wild,* a work that appeared with it in the *Miscellanies.* Part of the reason for its neglect lies in its format, purporting as it does to be the incomplete manuscript that a lodger left behind in lieu of rent in the garret of a stationer in the Strand. The eighteenth century was, to be sure, more accustomed to this kind of fictitious device than is our own age, but it is still a difficult one to deal with, and it is tempting to accept the view of Fielding's biographer, Wilbur Cross, that the novelist knew that the relation of Julian's adventures was growing tedious and deliberately brought the work to a rapid conclusion by the familiar device of an incomplete manuscript. F. Homes Dudden in his more recent study follows the same basic line of argument but with a more clearly asserted judgment of Fielding's intention: "It seems evident that Fielding commenced his tale with enthusiasm, but, in the course of recounting the metamorphoses of Julian, lost interest in his subject, meandered on for a while without any clearly defined design, and at last gave it up as a bad job."[9] Despite these opinions, however, a large measure of thematic and artistic integrity is recognizable in the work.

The *Journey* may be divided into four parts, each of which helps to achieve Fielding's thematic objectives: Part 1, consisting of the first six chapters of book 1, concerns the passage of the soul from the body after death, and details its journey to the gate of Elysium, which is presided over by the judge, Minos; part 2, the seventh to the ninth chapters of the first book, describes the narrator's experiences with Minos and those immediately following his passage into Elysium; part 3, chapters ten to twenty-five of the first book, narrates the adventures of Julian the Apostate during his numerous returns to earth, a section that is broken off supposedly because of the defectiveness of the manuscript; and, finally, part 4, chapter seven of book 19, tells the story of Anna Boleyn, which gives Fielding an opportunity to consider those vanities of women, and those desires for advancement in position and wealth among them, that are not far different from the ambitions of Julian.

Thematically, the book deals with subjects that form the thrust of Fielding's thinking in most of what he wrote during this period: the relationship between action and motive, the pervading pragmatism of human thinking, the absence of concern for the welfare of others, and the pretense that cloaks vice under the guise of virtue. In the *Journey,* the reader confronts death where all pretense and deceit are unmasked and sees death, as life itself, as a trip in which the soul must be purified and stripped of any residue of fleshly concerns and passions.

Jonathan Wild

Fielding's dissection of greatness and goodness is the central focus of his other major work of this period, *Jonathan Wild.* Capitalizing on the well-known life of the famous criminal who had been hanged in 1725, Fielding fictionalizes his biography adding elements that serve to define his concept of greatness and goodness.

Jonathan Wild is the story of a master criminal who has organized the thieves, pickpockets, and other petty felons of London to steal property which he himself arranges to return to its owners for a reward close to its original value. Wild disciplines the thieves by his ability to work with the authorities and have the criminals impeached and, in many cases, hanged, if they should disregard his orders. He is helped in this work by Geoffrey Snap, who arrests individuals for debt or petty offenses, and confines them at his own house until they either provide bail or security, or are directed to Newgate Prison. At his house Snap divests those arrested of what money they have by permitting gambling, by the charging of fees, and by the expert use of his two daughters, Laetitia and Theodocia. Among the prisoners Wild meets Count La Ruse, with whom he forms a close friendship. Their mutual respect is the result of their ability to steal from each other undetected. Working together, they undertake the destruction of Heartfree, a former schoolmate of Wild, but an individual who has led an exemplary and honest life as a jewelry merchant.

Wild and La Ruse accomplish the ruin of Heartfree by robbing him of his jewelry and having him arrested for debt. Heartfree's wife and children are thus left destitute, and Wild, seeking to seduce the wife, tricks her into taking a voyage with him to Holland under the guise of selling jewels to effect the release of her husband. His attempted rape of her during a storm at sea results in his being set adrift by the captain in an open boat, but he succeeds in returning to London, where he devotes himself to the task of having Heartfree hanged by having him falsely accused of sending his wife out of the country with his jewelry in order to avoid his creditors.

Wild, after many efforts to woo Laetitia Snap, is successful in marrying her, but their marriage is a turbulent one. Finally, Wild is himself arrested, as is Laetitia, and they quarrel in prison, while still plotting the destruction of Heartfree. Fortunately, Mrs. Heartfree, after many adventures, returns to London in time to save her husband from the gallows. Moreover, she has recovered the stolen jewelry and has added to it a magnificent jewel that assures their economic independence. Wild, on the other hand, is sent to the gallows, as his former friends and associates turn against him.

Wild and Heartfree form contrasting pictures of greatness and goodness. Fielding's conception of greatness is not in conflict with that of the world. The problem lies in the disjunction that Fielding establishes between greatness and goodness. Greatness in the world is, in fact, associated with power and wealth. In this sense, the poor, the humble, and the trusting are seldom among the great. The world judges the great by these standards, but at the same time assumes that those who manifest surface appearances of greatness also possess goodness. Thus kings, and statesmen, and squires, and bishops, and generals, and all men of position appear to the world as both great and good. Fielding's point is that the great take pains to put on a cloak of virtue to cover the corruption that often flourishes underneath. He suggests that although it is difficult and often impossible for men of great position to possess those characteristics that constitute goodness, they are, by the very power of their office, able to present themselves to the world in a manner that creates the illusion of goodness.

Hypocrisy is the dominant characteristic of Wild, and that which enables him to succeed. In the last chapter of *Jonathan Wild* Fielding lists fifteen of the maxims set forth by Wild "as the certain methods of attaining greatness." Number twelve of these perhaps suggests the thrust of all of them: "That virtues, like precious stones, were easily counterfeited; that the counterfeits in both cases adorned the wearer equally, and that very few had knowledge or discernment sufficient to distinguish the counterfeit jewel from the real." Ultimately, the possession of power and position is not in itself corrupt, but the effort to use them hypocritically to hide the corruption buried beneath them is.

Much the same may be said of goodness, and true goodness is not to be associated with all those qualities ordinarily recognized as virtues. For Fielding, charity, which is the outgrowth of good nature, is the determining characteristic of the good, much as hypocrisy is the salient characteristic of the great. Just as the great man may possess many attributes that in themselves are neutral or good in certain circumstances, but that are made corrupt by deceit, so too the good man may be guilty of acts that are generally regarded as vices, but that in balance do not prevent him from doing good if that individual possesses real concern for his fellowman.

Wild, a master of fraud, pretends to be Heartfree's friend; he works with Count La Ruse as each of them deceives the other; he pretends to love Laetitia; and seems to have bonds of loyalty with Trap and with members of his gang. Moreover, a key feature of his successful occupation is his ability to appear to conduct a business that is beneficial to the public, and to create the illusion of helping society by the apprehension of criminals. Wild can take advantage of Heartfree only by appearing to be Heartfree's friend, a pose he maintains throughout the novel, even while plotting the final destruction of the merchant. Moreover, he extends his pretense to his dealings with Mrs. Heartfree and imposes on her credulity to persuade her to take the projected trip to Holland. On the other hand, Heartfree is vulnerable because he is open and honest in his dealings and because he possesses a real concern for others. Deceit is inimical to true charity just as openness can never exist in the hypocritical individual.

Heartfree is one of the "silly" people, as Fielding ironically describes them. He is of an "honest and open disposition" and has several "great weaknesses of mind, being good-natured, friendly, and generous to a great excess." In his business dealings he also rejects common business ethics, for he has "forgiven some debts to his acquaintance only because they could not pay him"; he never takes advantage of the ignorance of his customers and is satisfied "with very moderate gains on his goods" (bk. 2, chap. 1). But with all his charity and honesty, Thomas Heartfree is a successful

jeweler before he meets Wild, and it is the deliberate malevolence of Wild
that undoes him. In all respects, Heartfree is the opposite of his supposed
friend, and this is one of the reasons Wild comes to hate him.

Fielding contrasts greatness and goodness in the marriages of Wild and
Heartfree and demonstrates how their ruling passions influence not only
their choice of mate but their happiness. The marriage of Wild presents an
example of ridiculous pretense; that of Heartfree, one of ecstatic,
sentimental bliss. Wild's pursuit of Laetitia Snap is filled with difficulties.
He is an awkward lover and little understands how to woo a woman.
Fielding relishes describing the "chaste" Laetitia in her "most beautiful
undress," in which her garments do not match and are marked by holes
that testify to their antique character. Wild also has two rivals for the
affections of the tattered beauty—the beau, Tom Smirk, and the thief,
Bagshot. The conversation between Laetitia and Wild in chapter 9 of book
1 ends with Wild fighting off Tishy's repeated blows and being forced to
withdraw in anger: "Wild now retreated from the conflict, and the
victorious Laetitia, with becoming triumph and noble spirit cried out,
'D--n your eyes, if this be your way of showing your love, I'll warrant I
gives you enough on't.' She then proceeded to talk of her virtue, which
Wild bid her carry to the devil with her, and thus our lovers parted." The
reader learns the true nature of Laetitia's supposed virtue as she quickly lets
Tom Smirk out of a closet where he had taken refuge upon the arrival of
Wild, and proceeds to make Smirk "as happy as Wild desired to be" (bk.
1, chap. 9). Wild finally marries Laetitia after setting down strict premarital conditions, and they arrive at a *modus operandi* for living together a
fortnight after their wedding, deciding to "henceforwards never live like
man and wife; that is, never be loving nor ever quarrel" (bk. 3, chap. 8).
Their final meeting is in Newgate where each expresses the fervent desire
to see the other hanged.

Their relationship differs markedly from that of Heartfree and his wife,
who live together in great trust and harmony. Even in the greatest of
distresses they respond to each other's needs in a selfless manner. When,
for example, Heartfree is robbed by Wild's gang of the one thousand
pounds given him by Count La Ruse, his wife does all she can to raise
money to replace it, and, though unsuccessful, she is careful not to
reproach or torment him. On the day in question, "She found him sealing
the last of several letters, which he was dispatching to his friends and
creditors. The moment he saw her a sudden joy sparkled in his eyes,
which, however, had a very short duration; for despair soon closed them
again; nor could he help bursting into some passionate expressions of

concern for her and his little family, which she, on her part, did her utmost to lessen, by endeavoring to mitigate the loss, and to raise in him hopes from the count, who might, she said, be possibly only gone into the country" (bk. 2, chap. 7).

Fielding's portrait of Heartfree is in the tradition of the kind of sentimentalism that had entered into the drama at the turn of the century and found its strong expression in George Lillo's *London Merchant* and, later on, in Edward Moore's *The Gamester*. As in Richard Steele's *The Conscious Lovers,* it focuses on the good merchant, but it departs from Steele to emphasize distress in family life. In advancing a sentimental view of good nature, it has a kinship with the sentimentalism of Richard Cumberland's great comedy, *The West Indian.* Although sentimentalism in the drama moved in a variety of directions, the common elements of the idealization of an honest merchant, an emphasis on the loyalty of true friendship, the potential for connubial bliss, and the presence of alien forces prepared to interrupt and perhaps destroy the efforts of the good are common to most dramas of the type. By the time Fielding wrote *Jonathan Wild,* the novel had not yet evolved to a point at which one could recognize the tradition of sentiment as it existed in the theater. Richardson, whose first novel could be regarded as sentimental, hardly fits the mold of sentimentalism as it was emerging in the drama.

By means of the Heartfree story, Fielding uses the tradition of sentimentalism to demonstrate how criminals like Wild and his confederates victimize the virtuous members of society. Heartfree is only one of a number of stock sentimental characters in the novel. Friendly, similar to the loyal servant of the dramatic tradition, manifests his great loyalty to his master, and at the same time contrasts with Wild's own disloyal confederates. Mrs. Heartfree is the long-suffering and supportive wife who stands by her husband whatever the difficulties he encounters and cares for their children in model fashion. Heartfree, himself, is the honest merchant, the epitome of the successful and ethical businessman, who goes through life not only as a model of goodness to his family and community, but one who deals charitably with his fellowman, particularly with those of his customers who find themselves in financial difficulty.

While it is valuable to recognize the series of opposite characteristics to be found in Heartfree and his family as compared to Wild, Laetitia, and their associates, the introduction of the Heartfree episode was not needed to develop Fielding's comparison of Wild with the great man of politics, Walpole. Perhaps too much has been made of Walpole as the object of Fielding's irony, and the suggestion that Wild is the ironic portrait of the prime minister. At the time the novel appeared, Walpole and Wild had been compared often in the opposition press, and the term "Great Man" had long been an ironic synonym for Walpole. Fielding, moreover, in the revision of the book completed just before his death, eliminated most of the references to prime minister and substituted "statesman," since it was clear that by that time the reference to Walpole had little satiric value. Of two entire chapters eliminated in the revision, one was substantially political in its nature. The novel, ultimately, says much more about human nature than it does about Walpole, and, as such, it deserves to be read. The Heartfree section of the story is the main means Fielding uses to shift the emphasis of the story away from a narrow political satire, and toward a wide-ranging comment on the selfish hypocrisy of mankind.

In using the established picture of Walpole as a Great Man identified with Wild, Fielding knew that the immediacy of Walpole's fall, and the general condemnation he was at that time experiencing, were far more current in the public eye than the career of Wild that had come to an end seventeen years before. For this reason, Walpole functions rhetorically as a means of describing the danger posed for society by Wild, rather than Wild suggesting the dangers inherent in the career of the prime minister. Many of Fielding's readers were aware of the master criminal merely as a legend, but the invidious features of Walpole's character had been widely trumpeted by the triumphant opposition and were very much in the public mind. Because of this the dangers that the power of Walpole held for the state and for the people could be seen to be not unlike the dangers posed for society by the presence of master criminals like Wild, who possess the same character flaws as Walpole and are equally dangerous. Fielding brilliantly uses the currency of the feeling of distaste for the "greatness" of Walpole to demonstrate the dangerous power of the petty great man or criminal preying on society. In accomplishing this, the character of Heartfree and Wild's attempt to destroy him have their greatest importance.

An important feature of serious sentimental drama came to be the malevolent and psychologically distorted motivation of the villain. In *The London Merchant*, Millwood, who has a paranoid view of men, moves against the inexperienced and naive Barnwell, because only through him can she wreak proper vengeance on the male sex. In *The Gamester* of Edward Moore, Stukely seeks to destroy Beverly because the latter has married the woman whom Stukely loved. Such psychologically depraved motivation is similar to that of Wild in pursuing the destruction of Heartfree. Wild does not want merely to cheat Heartfree, but to destroy him, and for reasons that can bring no logically sane benefit to Wild. Heartfree must be robbed, he must be destroyed, he must be imprisoned, his wife must be raped, and he must be hanged. This is Wild's depraved motivation, and the measure of his villainy. In developing these motives in Wild, Fielding departs greatly from his ironic portrait of Walpole, who, as a corrupt politician, little resembles the personally vicious character attributed to Wild in his dealing with Heartfree. For this reason, the novel takes on a significance far broader than political satire.

Fielding is interested in both Walpole and Wild as popular images of greatness, images that are not very different from those that history has drawn of Alexander, Caesar, and other great conquerors of the past. Fielding analyzes the factors that separate goodness from greatness in the public estimate of the actions of men, just as he had in *Shamela, Joseph Andrews,* and *A Journey from this World to the Next.* Wild does not possess "greatness" because he is a thief, any more than Walpole does because he is a politician. Both men are "great" because they live totally selfish lives, pursue individual success in their professions without regard to the lives or rights of others, and unashamedly pursue the destruction of anyone whose interest conflicts with theirs. The possession of power by whatever means achieved, moreover, carries with it a large measure of popular acceptance because power permits the individual possessing it to project a favorable image of himself and his actions through pretense and deceit. The great man, whether Wild or Walpole, pretends to act through good motives and finds acceptance because the motives of such a large portion of the world are similar to his.

In the cross section of life presented by Fielding as he describes Wild and his associates, Wild's values are not rejected, although few if any can pursue them with the same intensity. Count La Ruse, Snap, Laetitia, Theodosia, Fireblood, and Blueskin all value life in terms consistent with those of Wild. Even the chaplain of Newgate easily succumbs to the flattery and logic of Wild, and drinking a bowl of punch together becomes a substitute for religion.

Newgate, toward the end of the novel, becomes a microcosmic version of the world at large, as the great man Wild serves to corrupt those he meets there, especially the debtors:

But we have, already, perhaps, detained our reader too long in this relation from the consideration of our hero, who daily gave the most exalted proofs of greatness in cajoling the *prigs,* and in exactions on the debtors; which latter now grew so great, *i.e.,* corrupted in their morals, that they spoke with the utmost contempt of what the vulgar call honesty. The greatest character among them was that of a pickpocket, or in truer language, a *file*; and the only censure was want of dexterity. As to virtue, goodness, and such like, they were the objects of mirth and derision, and all Newgate was a complete collection of *prigs*, every man being desirous to pick his neighbor's pocket, and every one was as sensible that his neighbor was as ready to pick his; so that (which is almost incredible) as great roguery daily was committed within the walls of Newgate as without. (bk. 4, chap. 12)

While Wild's corruption of the debtors in Newgate can be viewed as analogous to Walpole's corruption of government through the power of his office, the scene has truth and validity apart from any reference to the prime minister. Eighteenth-century English prisons did in fact function in a way that promoted the corruption of those incarcerated in them. Fielding's picture of prison life in *Amelia,* a more direct and reliable one than that in *Jonathan Wild,* is not substantially different, although the great men within its walls might not be as skillful practitioners of the criminal arts as is Wild. In *Jonathan Wild* Fielding discusses the corruption of the people of the world at large by the master criminal as much as he considers the corruption of the people of the political world by the prime minister.

Fielding focuses on goodness as well as greatness, and he emphasizes, as he had in *Joseph Andrews,* that example works effectively on the reader. The power of example is a recognized force in the tradition of sentiment, manifested in the drama by the fifth-act scene of repentance in which the temporarily corrupt hero is snatched from a life of vice by perceiving the model goodness of his beloved. So great was the impact of the story of George Barnwell in *The London Merchant* as an emblem of virtuous youth corrupted and redeemed that viewing Lillo's play was recommended for young apprentices. In *Jonathan Wild* Heartfree, his wife, and Friendly are models of virtue set before the reader as an alternative to the pursuit of greatness. The two paths described in *A Journey from this World to the Next* are still possible alternatives, even though a majority seem to prefer the allurements of the craggy road to greatness.

Fielding's use of sustained irony from the beginning to the end of the novel is a complicated and difficult technique. From the point of view of craftsmanship, *Jonathan Wild* is a masterpiece and demonstrates the novelist's recognition of the relationship that exists between form and matter in structuring the book. What occurs is not the inversion of greatness and goodness but the unrelenting portrayal of the world's conception of these two characteristics of human life, stripped of the comforting colorations of pretense. Greatness is both material success in the world and the ability to pursue that success with undiverted diligence; goodness is moral virtue exercised through intimate interaction between individuals. This scheme of things allows no room for pretense as an alternative to true virtue. Fielding's sentimentalized portrait of Heartfree and his family makes possible the unmasking of pretense. Unadorned virtue, unreserved affection, genuine honesty, and generous charity appear as exaggerations only because the world at large confuses the nature of goodness and greatness. The technical perfection of Fielding's sustained portrayal of the difference between truth and the common perception of truth is the result of an irony that actually exists in life, rather than something created by the novelist. Fielding, largely through the introduction of Heartfree into Wild's life, enables the reader to perceive and accept this essential irony in a manner that would not be possible through direct statement.

Fielding maintains the reader's attention by creating key scenes that are comic in the vision of the ridiculous they create, and they produce genuine laughter. Fielding juxtaposes two scenes in rapid succession, one in which Bagshot, who has, at the instigation of Wild, robbed Count La Ruse of money he had won at the gaming table from Wild, is confronted by Wild and forced to relinquish three-fourths of his booty; the other, in which Laetitia Snap fends off the advances of Wild largely because Tom Smirk is hidden in the closet. Wild's ability to deal with one of his own type, Bagshot, is counterbalanced by his inability to deal with Laetitia, who knows how to deal with men and is able to use that ability to make a fool of the master criminal. Wild understands the requirements of greatness, the ability to selfishly pursue his own ends, but when he finds himself in circumstances different from those in which he customarily works, he is unable to apply his principle of greatness effectively. He cannot use what he has learned among thieves and pickpockets to protect himself against a woman who uses the charms and instincts of her sex to gull him. The result is a portrayal of the ridiculous that prompts comic laughter. Although Wild is similarly blunted in his pursuit of greatness by Molly Straddle, who takes from him, in the midst of their amorous caresses, the very money he had arranged to have stolen from Heartfree, he is able to use matters to his advantage when Molly makes the error of attempting to have Heartfree change the five-hundred pound note she had taken from Wild. Heartfree's recognition of the note enables Wild to blackmail Molly into giving evidence against one of Wild's gang, Fierce, whom the master criminal wants to eliminate because he has objected to giving over most of what he steals. Wild also convinces his confederate Sly to do the same. Wild thus demonstrates his true greatness by using the lie of Molly Straddle and Sly's betrayal of his friend to bring Fierce to the gallows.

Fielding had become a master of dialogue during his theatrical career and had learned to use it as an instrument for characterization. The conversation between Wild and Laetitia two weeks after their wedding reveals the extent to which each despises the other, while it demonstrates their practical ability to arrange a pact under which they can live with each other successfully. The same talent is displayed as Fielding makes an original character of the chaplain of Newgate, giving him a unique personality while still having him manifest the general deficiencies of the inadequate clergymen of the day. At the same time, he allows Wild, through his exchange with him, to reveal further the rationalistic view of life that prevents him from being moved to any sort of repentance. Before the clergyman's attempt to bring the criminal to a sense of his relationship to his Maker is completed, he becomes as much a man of the world as Wild himself. After offering an extended opinion as to why Wild should meet his death as an expiation for his sins, the following dialogue ensues:

> *Jonathan.* All this is very true; but let us take a bottle of wine to cheer our spirits.
>
> *Ordinary.* Why wine? Let me tell you, Mr. Wild, there is nothing so deceitful as the spirits given us by wine. If you must drink, let us have a bowl of punch—a liquor I the rather prefer, as it is nowhere spoken against in scripture, and as it is more wholesome for the gravel, a distemper with which I am grievously afflicted.
>
> *Jonathan.* (*having called for a bowl*). I ask your pardon, doctor; I should have remembered that punch was your favorite liquor. I think you never taste wine while there is any punch remaining on the table.
>
> *Ordinary.* I confess I look on punch to be the more eligible liquor, as well for the reasons I have before mentioned as likewise for one other cause, it is the properest for a DRAUGHT. I own I took it a little unkind of you to mention wine, thinking you knew my palate.   (bk. 4, chap. 13)

The conversation continues in sociable fashion with the chaplain delivering a sermon on foolishness and Wild receiving it by lapsing into a quiet sleep until the arrival of the punch puts an end to the sermon of the one and the sleep of the other. The clergyman, caught up in the trappings of religion, is unable to do more than offer the series of formulas that his prepared text and written sermons have provided him. Wild continues his unflinching pursuit of his own comforts with a civility that demonstrates the admirable control of the great man. Through a brilliant and delicate use of satiric dialogue Fielding advances the portraits of the two men.

Wild is in the final analysis a failure. He goes to the gallows, not in triumph, but to the jeers of the multitude, unable in his last moments to take his own life by the ingestion of laudanum, as his rebellious spirit vomits the narcotic. While often able to destroy petty criminals, and, for a time, almost successful in bringing about the complete destruction of Heartfree and his family. Wild is characterized at the end by an inability to control himself.

His own vanity and inability to sense the value or significance of other people prevents Wild from seeing how fortune has destroyed him. This is the road to greatness, craggy, fraught with disasters, but desirable because of the power it temporarily offers to those who travel it. The pursuers of greatness, through their very ruthlessness, are able to victimize, at least in this world, those who follow the path to goodness. For this reason, Wild, as created by Fielding, is less important than his victim, Heartfree. What could have been merely another satiric attack on Walpole, or on the great in political life, becomes a social lesson that develops a thesis concerning the impact of the unrestrained criminal on the lesser members of society, many of whom would not be criminal were it not for his questionable organizational talents. In examining the impact of Wild on society, it is instructive to recall the portrait of Cardinal Wolsey as drawn by Fielding in the seemingly innocuous last segment of *A Journey from this World to the Next*. It is the great man, Cardinal Wolsey, who first begins the corruption of Anne Boleyn, and it is he who fans in her father the latent sparks for material success. Caught between the servile willingness of Wolsey to please Henry VIII, even if it means violating all the religious principles for which his office stands, and the more understandable but equally destructive ambition of her father, Anne succumbs to her own love of pomp and circumstance.

If the total thrust of Fielding's creative output during the period in which *Jonathan Wild* appeared is kept in mind, the novel seems less directed against Walpole as a political enemy than designed to set up the position of prime minister as an emblem of the general penchant of mankind for greatness, a goal marked by greed and a lust for power, and achieved through deceit. This seems an appropriate reading of even the earlier version of the novel, before the satire was modified to make it less offensive to the prime minister.

Fielding has taken the reader from the assault on the venality and deception inherent in Pamela and Parson Williams in *Shamela*; through the more positive portrait of virtue in *Joseph Andrews* in the persons of Parson Adams, Joseph, and Fanny, and the less literary evaluation of goodness inherent in the judgment of Minos in *A Journey from this World to the Next*; to a final culmination in *Jonathan Wild,* in which the contrasting portraits of greatness and goodness in Wild and Heartfree give insights into the corruptive force of greatness on the individual and into the potential of the great man in all walks of life to destroy those who follow the path of goodness.

Chapter Four
The Mature Novelist: *Tom Jones*

From the time of its initial publication *Tom Jones* has been a controversial novel, with diverse opinion centering on two factors that are extraneous to the work itself: the political situation in which Fielding found himself at the time of its publication and the moral character of the book. The political question has been less a problem in the enjoyment of the work in the years since the immediate period during which it appeared, for the circumstances surrounding the attempted restoration of the Stuarts to the throne in 1745 quickly passed into history when the effort failed, making no permanent impact on English history. The events of that year, however, provided an excellent and fruitful setting for the novel, which served to provide the tale with a temporal realism, and to reveal how politics tangentially influences individual lives, while more provincial concerns remain paramount. Tom, for example, almost becomes directly involved in the rebellion, as he joins a group of soldiers heading for the conflict. More immediate concerns, however, intervene before this is accomplished when his fight with Ensign Northerton delays his journey north. He finally forgets all his promises to join the battle when he learns that Sophia is on her way to London, and he sets out in pursuit of her. Similarly, although the politics of Partridge and Tom are basically different, the two men manage to be amiable companions once they meet on the road to London. The impact of politics on the popularity of the novel, moreover, had little to do with the substance of the book, and much of the adverse reaction in the press was due to Fielding's strong anti-government position during the Walpole administration, and his having contributed to the political journalism concerning the Stuart invasion in the pages of the *True Patriot* and the *Jacobite's Journal*.

Of greater long-range difficulty has been the moral structure of *Tom Jones* and the failure of readers to distinguish between the moral convictions of Fielding and the actions of his main characters in the novel. The moral import of *A Journey from this World to the Next* is easy to grasp as charity and acts of positive good to one's neighbor become criteria for salvation. The work is illustrative of an ideal easily accepted once it is recognized. Even the case of Anne Boleyn is clearly explained, and she is saved only because she has been, while on earth, punished for her crimes. The rhetorical use of allegory and fiction in the *Journey* is far different from the aesthetic use of those elements in *Tom Jones*. In the novel, Fielding does not emerge as a judge of human conduct, but as a historian revealing the complex fabric of the human ethical dilemma. For this reason, the philosophical moralist finds the work confusing, for just as in life an understanding of people's motives is essential to a moral judgment of what they do, and such motives are often not easily ascertained, so too, in the world of Fielding's fiction, motives are often obscure and moral evaluation difficult. While the objections Samuel Richardson makes to the novel are often petty,[1] those of the more disinterested critic Samuel Johnson need to be considered. In Johnson's view, the work has little to recommend it, since it deals with low characters and a morally offensive hero.[2] Johnson's opinion has, unfortunately, continued to prevail in the popular mind, despite more enlightened recent scholarship. *Tom Jones* is still thought to be a racy book, and its hero something of a reformed rake.

The Plot

Much of the cause of the misunderstanding of the moral intent of *Tom Jones* lies in the plot itself,[3] which, when divorced from Fielding's satiric irony and approached by readers unaccustomed to the subtlety of his writing, presents the picture of a young man of loose sexual morals who is rescued in a deus ex machina fashion from a dissolute life to be unconvincingly saved by a beautiful heroine. Tom Jones is the illegitimate son of Bridget Allworthy, the sister of a Somersetshire squire who is a model of justice and charity. His father is a Mr. Summer, who dies of the smallpox before he and Bridget can marry. To conceal the truth of Tom's parentage, Bridget pays a young lady from a neighboring town, Jenny Jones, to quietly accept the guilt and to go into exile. Bridget arranges to leave her child at the doorstep of the affluent Allworthy, knowing that he, as a man of proven benevolence, will take her son into his house; and thus, although she publicly reviles Tom's parents, she provides well for him. A short time later Bridget marries Captain Blifil and gives birth to another son, eight months after their marriage. Tom and Master Blifil are, therefore, sons of the same mother but different fathers. Only an accident of fate makes Blifil in reality more legitimate than Tom, as both are brought up in the household of Allworthy. But the facts of Tom's birth are not known, and Blifil is regarded as the squire's nephew by blood, and Tom merely the object of his largess.

As Tom and Blifil grow up, their lives intertwine with those of Allworthy's neighbor, Squire Western, and his beautiful daughter, Sophia. Tom falls deeply in love with Sophia, and becomes a well-liked companion of Western, with whom he shares a love of hunting and whom he impresses with his great skill with both horse and gun. Tom is also revealed as an open, naturally charitable, and free-spirited youth, while Blifil develops traits of deceit and worldly ambition. Blifil's talent for pretense makes him appear the greater success in the eyes of most people, expecially the tutors of the young men, Thwackum and Square.

Living nearby are the gamekeeper, "Black George" Seagrim, and his daughter, Molly, both of whom like the ebullient and open nature of Tom. An illness that strikes Allworthy sharply alters the direction of the novel, and particularly the life of its hero. The squire, who was thought to be dying, suddenly revives, and this intelligence so pleases Tom that he drinks the squire's health to an immoderate degree and, in the midst of his joy, is drawn into the thickest part of a neighboring grove by Molly Seagrim and succumbs to her seductive wiles. This scene is witnessed by Thwackum and Blifil and reported to Allworthy in such a way that he interprets it as a mark of Tom's ingratitude. Deeply hurt, he banishes Tom from his estate, bringing to an end the first section of the novel, and opening the way for the young man's journey to London.

Tom's adventures on his way to London are a fascinating series of experiences. He sets out penniless, despite the fact that Allworthy had given him a five-hundred pound note when he left. Not aware of its value, Tom carelessly loses it, only to have it found by Black George, who keeps it. He has with him, to be sure, a purse from Sophia containing the sixteen guineas she has been able to save, but to Tom this is a sacred trust to be returned to her, and not to be used.

Seeing no other way to survive, Tom decides to go to sea, but, encountering a company of soldiers on their way to fight the Stuart invaders, he decides to accompany them. En route he meets Ensign Northerton, quarrels with him, and is wounded. A local barber, Partridge, doubling as a surgeon, treats Tom's injuries, and together they set out to overtake the soldiers. The barber eventually turns out to be the neighbor whom Allworthy, twenty years before, had suspected of being Tom's father, and consequently had forced to leave that part of England. While on the road with Partridge, Tom rescues a local man from a band of robbers, and this loquacious individual is the Man of the Hill, whose story forms one of the important digressions of the novel.

Tom, who, like Parson Adams, is prepared to rescue anyone in distress, saves a Mrs. Waters from Ensign Northerton's attempt to rob her, and takes her under his protection. Unknown to him, she is Jenny Jones, who, like Partridge, had been forced to flee on account of the circumstances surrounding Tom's birth. Tom, Mrs. Waters, and Partridge find their way to an inn at Upton, which becomes a pivotal location for the action of the novel. A series of often ludicrous or sentimental scenes occur that are of great importance in the evolution of the tale. The most comic of these scenes is the mock-epic battle in which Tom Jones, Partridge, and Mrs. Waters battle with the landlord, the landlady, and their maid, Susan, in hilarious fashion.

Most of the important characters in the novel find their way to the inn at this time, but not always with the knowledge of one another. A Mrs. Fitzpatrick, who figures importantly later in the story, arrives and leaves just before Squire Western. Tom yields to the amorous advances of Mrs. Waters only to have his actions later discovered by Sophia, who, having left home to avoid an arranged marriage with Blifil, is on her way to London to seek the protection of Lady Bellaston, a distant relative. His encounter with Mrs. Waters is later to have a profound impact on Tom when he learns that she is thought to be his mother, and he believes that he has been unwittingly guilty of incest. Learning of Tom's escapade, Sophia leaves a muff on his bed with her name attached to it. When he recognizes it, he impetuously leaves in rapid pursuit of her. Sophia and her party, meanwhile, meet an Irish peer, a friend of Mrs. Fitzpatrick, and they continue the journey to London in his coach.

All the principals eventually arrive in London, and the action of the final third of the novel centers around the lodgings of Lady Bellaston, to whom Sophia, a distant relation, goes for help. Soon after coming to London, Tom meets and enters into an amour with Lady Bellaston. When chance brings him into Sophia's presence at Lady Bellaston's home, Tom is terrified lest Sophia learn that he is being kept by the Lady. Eventually he extricates himself from his relationship with Lady Bellaston by offering her an insincere proposal of marriage knowing that she will reject it. While in London, Tom experiences other significant adventures. He takes a lodging with Mrs. Miller, an honest woman who always keeps a room ready for Squire Allworthy, and while Tom is there, the young man generously befriends the family of Mrs. Miller's cousin and saves her daughter, Nancy, from being abandoned by Nightingale. On another occasion, Tom finds himself involved with Mrs. Fitzpatrick's husband, and the resulting duel in which Fitzpatrick is injured brings about Tom's imprisonment. Eventually, the truth of Tom's birth is discovered and he is reconciled to Allworthy, who learns of Blifil's treachery. Tom and Sophia are happily united.

The Structure of *Tom Jones*

A recitation of the central facts of the tale does little to reveal the artistic and aesthetic whole which conveys Fielding's intuitive view of life.[4] On the other hand, it provides a framework for understanding the irony and satire by which Fielding strips character after character of his vanities. Similarly, the careful overall structure of the novel and the meticulous way in which it is put together form an appropriate contrast to the accidental way in which many circumstances seem to occur. Ultimately these events are shown to be essential to the story and to result from well-designed motivation.

Tom Jones is divided into eighteen books, six of which are devoted to each of the three main sections of the work. Following the pattern established in *Joseph Andrews,* the novel is centered in two locations, linked by a journey of the principal characters from one to the other, this time reversing the pattern, with the action beginning in the country and ending in London. Starting with the introduction of the chief people in the story and the essential circumstances of their lives, the first section contains sufficient detail to establish both the personality and ethical character of these individuals. The ingredients are thus introduced to prepare the way for the eventual resolution of the plot in the last section of the novel. Tom is early revealed as open, honest, and concerned with the feelings of others when he rescues Sophia's bird, while Blifil is quickly recognized as both spiteful and deceitful when he maliciously releases it on the pretense that he is providing freedom to one of God's creatures. Tom's fundamental grasp of the importance of charity emerges in his kindness to Black George and his family, while his amoral sexual ethics, typified in his relationship with Molly Seagrim, represents a flaw in his character that will be further aggravated by his association with Mrs. Waters and Lady Bellaston before being sentimentally purified by the moral perfection of Sophia.

The character of Allworthy is also established early, in preparation for his role in the closing section of the novel in which the fabric of corruption woven by Blifil is unraveled. Allworthy suffers from an inadequacy caused by his own goodness when he judges the actions of others. Not trained in the law or judicial process, he must function as Justice of the Peace in his locality and be responsible for the maintenance of order in his part of the country. Allworthy lacks the cynicism needed to judge motives and, for this reason, tends to read literally evidence that is presented under the mask of pretense. He fails to recognize Bridget's possible guilt in the vigor of her condemnation of Tom's mother as "an impudent slut, a wanton hussy, an audacious harlot, a wicked jade, a vile strumpet," and similar epithets (bk. 1, chap. 4). The overkill of her expression might well have alerted a more cynical person to the possibility of her own involvement. Allworthy's condemnation of Jenny Jones is more understandable, for she offers no defense, and he shows a prudent concern for her need to survive by allowing her to establish a new identity in another locality where her supposed indiscretion would be unknown. On the other hand, his condemnation of the innocent Partridge on the strength of the perjured testimony of his wife is evidence of almost culpable credulity. He did not understand, as did Fielding, the wisdom of the law "which refuses to admit the evidence of a wife for or against her husband" (bk. 2, chap. 6). It is this same inability to sort out motives and evidence that causes Allworthy to condemn Tom and thus set in motion all the disastrous consequences that follow. It is also, however, Allworthy's fundamental honesty and his dedication to truth and to justice that enable him to reverse his judgment in the presence of contrary evidence at the conclusion of the book.

The central third of the novel is devoted to the passage of the principal figures from the country to London. In the brief time the journey takes, a little more than a week, Fielding uses the experiences Tom encounters to bring about a marked maturation in him and to prepare him for a sobering month before the true facts of his birth are made known, the falsity of the accusations against him revealed, and his love for Sophia brought to a happy result. Fielding's problem was not only to bring Tom and Sophia to London, but also to arrange for the appearance there of the many other personages whose lives crossed Tom's and whose presence was essential to the establishment of his innocence. The key meeting that Tom has with Partridge, his supposed father, as a result of his fight with Ensign Northerton, places the other single most aggrieved individual in the young man's company. Tom also meets on the way his supposed mother, Jenny Jones, in her new identity as Mrs. Waters, and his sexual involvement with her would have been a careless incestuous act had she really been his mother. Tom, to be sure, is unaware of the identity of Mrs. Waters, but Sophia's discovery of the incident and her letting him know that she knows of it (by leaving her muff behind for him to find) have a significant effect on him. It so intensifies his passion for Sophia that Tom completely forgets his pledge to join the military and sets off in pursuit of his true love. Mrs. Waters, like Molly Seagrim, is no true object of Tom's love, but merely the means of satisfying a brief moment of passion. The intensity of Tom's reaction to the discovery of the muff serves to affirm the strength of his love for Sophia, just as his abandonment of Lady Bellaston and the material advantages of their liaison later in the novel demonstrates his commitment to Sophia. Moreover, when he discovers, while in prison, that he may well have been guilty of incest, the consequences of his promiscuity are made clear to him.

Jones's sexual activity is essentially amoral and his reform requires the kind of social maturation that only experience can provide. The consequences of his entanglements with the three women are progressively less serious in terms of his personal survival, but increasingly more serious in their threat to his romantic position with Sophia. Her capacity to understand what happened between Tom and Molly results from a knowledge of men, born of her observation of her father's crude and earthy approach to life. The discovery of Tom's affair with Mrs. Waters is a more serious breach, however, and her leaving her muff behind is both a rebuke to Tom and a test of his affection. The potential harm of his sustained relationship with Lady Bellaston is only set in perspective by his direct action to extricate himself from involvement with her. Tom takes on characteristics of the fallen lover of the sentimental tradition, falling progressively further into the mire in a way that demands an ever increasing understanding by the innocent beloved, until circumstances so develop that the reform of the hero is achieved by his recognition of his fault when his degradation is juxtaposed against the goodness and perfection of his heroic lady. In *Tom Jones* the devotion of an unmarried woman is tested; in his last novel, *Amelia,* Fielding will test the fortitude of devoted innocence in marriage.

The trip to London also tests the tenacity of Sophia's love. Her response to a series of circumstances reveals her extraordinary love for Tom, beginning with her sending him all the money she possesses when he is sent away. Her determination to avoid marriage to Blifil further reveals her devotion, while it sets her on the road to London. Her discovery of Tom and Mrs. Waters offers another challenge to her love. Sophia's consistent reaction to Tom's encounters with women is to consider whether or not they represent a lack of fidelity to her or simply a male sexual adventure of no permanent consequence. Her reaction is neither that of Richardson's

Pamela, to accept Mr. B--'s indiscretions after their marriage with a firm sense that she must do so if the marriage is to survive, nor that of Richardson's Clarissa, who would prefer to pine away until death mercifully releases her from her long, self-inflicted torture. On the contrary, Sophia combines the best elements of both reactions, tenaciously holding to her love of Tom while she tests her true intentions. The process is one of a developing maturity that results in an intensification of Sophia's instinctive understanding of life and does not represent a major shift in sensibility. Tom, on the other hand, undergoes a significant change in attitude, and when he is finally permanently united with Sophia, he is possessed of an understanding of her true worth that would seem to preclude any relapse into his former flaccid attitudes. Moreover, Fielding assures the reader of the permanence of their relationship by revealing that Sophia will, in the future, have two children, who will be committed to the care of Parson Adams for their education.

All of the essential characters find themselves in London for the last third of the novel. Allworthy and Western and their families are present, along with Jenny Jones, Partridge, and Black George. Moreover, other characters appear who reveal something of Tom's character, serve in his maturation, or bring to light the truth about his life. Captain and Mrs. Fitzpatrick, Mrs. Miller, Nightingale, Parson Supple, and Lord Fellamar add vitality to the story even as it draws to a conclusion. Dowling appears in order to reveal that he had had the story of Tom's birth from Bridget. Both of Tom's parents are dead, and it is their absence that allows the story to unfold slowly, as some twenty years after the fact a series of circumstances, triggered by the malevolence of Blifil, evolve to reveal the truth about Tom's birth, and to destroy the half brother who had maliciously set Allworthy against the supposed foundling. Blifil, and to a lesser extent Thwackum and Square, who have never been able to understand the youthful energy of Tom nor the true significance of his natural charity and generosity, are brought to account in a resolution of affairs, magnificent in its handling of detail, but especially devastating in the ironical implications of Bridget's violent condemnation of Tom's mother in the opening pages of the novel.

Fielding follows the structure of the epic tradition and continues to write his comic epic in prose, using the same basic format that he had used in *Joseph Andrews*. His target is still the ridiculous as manifested through either vanity or hypocrisy. Unlike *Joseph Andrews,* however, where all the characters are touched by vanity, either of the benign sort, such as that seen in the touches of pride in Parson Adams or Joseph, or the more serious hypocritical vanity of Lady Booby, that vice plays only a small part in the main action of *Tom Jones*. Where characters such as Allworthy or Joseph fail, it is not through vanity and its inherent deceit, but through too sincere and open natures that make them foils for others. Fielding weds his social ideas to his theoretical use of the epic tradition and, as recent studies have shown, to the rich store of fictional romance with which the novelist was acquainted.[5]

The Moral Basis of the Novel

Allworthy's basis for action differs from that of Tom Jones, for in maintaining his moral and ethical standards which are of the highest order, the squire acts through a conscious judgment that he is right. Allworthy is motivated by Christian standards of justice, and, although false evidence or misinterpreted facts may lead him to erroneous conclusions, he has an active and charitable conscience. Tom, on the other hand, relies entirely on the innate goodness of his nature to provide a standard of conduct, and, although his charitable exuberance provides adequate guidance in many areas, his lack of explicit moral principles of action accounts for his serious shortcomings in dealing with women. Thwackum and Square, whose religion is more argumentative than substantive, have little effect as moral guides for Tom, and even though the rectitude of Allworthy functions as an excellent example in those instances where the Squire's judgment is called upon, as a bachelor heading a household he is not in a position to provide in his own character a satisfactory model for sexual conduct.

Fielding exposes the ridiculous in *Tom Jones* in more serious moral terms than in *Joseph Andrews*. The hypocritical actions of Blifil, the deceit of Bridget, the conspiracy with Jenny Jones, the lies of Mrs. Partridge, the theft of the bank note by Black George, and the actions of Lady Bellaston are deeds of the blackest kind. Each serves to preserve the reputation or position of the individual concerned, but each likewise has serious consequences for the lives of others. While the mood of the novel seems ebullient and appreciative of life, the mood proves deceptive when the reader looks beyond the surface of the comedy. The realism of the novel accounts for much of the high spirits, but it also heightens the human tragedy that threatens before the plot is resolved.

The Novel's Realism

Fielding's realism derives in large measure from the historical context in which the novel is set. Although its locale is documented to a great extent, with references to places obviously recognizable both in the countryside and in London, it is the historical tensions inherent in the 1745 rebellion and the possible success of Prince Charles's invasion that establishes a realistic pattern in the personal, social, and political lives of the characters. Tom's life would have taken a very different direction from what it did, had he persevered in his intentions to join the forces fighting in the north, but the political realities facing the nation were of less consequence to him than the personal tragedy that might have resulted had he not pursued Sophia to London. Fielding keeps the rebellion in front of the reader, not only by such significant detail as Tom's encounter with the soldiers, but by less important references like Sophia's being mistaken for Jenny Cameron, the mistress of Prince Charles. Moreover, frequent topical references to actual places, events, and living personalities, such as Tom's accompanying Mrs. Miller and Partridge to see Garrick in *Hamlet,* serve to provide a strong realistic base for the story. Just as in ordinary life, war and peace, political turmoil, and other such circumstances are part of the human condition, but are more background than substance in the important judgments individuals make about each other and about the actions that affect the permanent patterns of their lives.

Fielding's Use of Digressions

An important part of Fielding's technique is the introduction of digressions, and, as in *Joseph Andrews,* they contribute significantly to the total fabric of the novel. Not to be confused with minor incidents that are linked with the central story, the digressions bear little or no direct relationship to the central fable. The two major digressions, the story of the Man of the Hill and the history of Mrs. Fitzpatrick, occur during the journey of Tom and Sophia to London and concern the lives of individuals who are not part of the main design of the novel. They do, however, serve the important function of furthering the characterization of both Tom and Sophia, separately but in parallel ways.

Jones meets the Man of the Hill as the result of his being drawn to the top of Mazzard Hill, a scene that when lit by moonlight meets, at least for him, the requirements for the sublime and for the sentimental beauty of melancholy. "I wish I was at the Top of this hill"; declares Tom to his companion, Partridge, "it must certainly afford a most charming prospect, especially by this light; for the solemn gloom which the moon casts on all objects is beyond expression beautiful, especially to an imagination which is desirous of cultivating melancholy ideas" (bk. 8, chap. 10). They find themselves at last at the home of the Man of the Hill. Although he is temporarily away, his servant greets them, and the details he gives of the inhabitant of the house prepare them for the eccentricities of an unusual individual. Not only is his appearance odd, but he is a man of considerable age. Born in 1657, he provides a link between the present rebellion and the earlier turmoils concerning the monarchy that occurred in the late seventeenth century when the Duke of Monmouth threatened the crown of Charles II and later James II. The Man of the Hill, extremely tall with a long white beard, dressed in the skin of an ass, crude leather boots, and a cap, seems in his dress to symbolize his withdrawal from civilization to the extent that it is possible to do so. When Tom rescues him from a group of thugs who have assaulted him, the Man of the Hill becomes well disposed toward his visitors and consents to tell the curious Tom his life story.

Embittered by life, he desires nothing more than to withdraw from the inhumanity of his fellowman. His view of man is expressed in words that might have been uttered by Gulliver returned from the land of the Houyhnhnms: "Man alone, the king of this globe, the last and greatest work of the Supreme Being, below the sun; man alone hath basely dishonoured his own nature, and by dishonesty, cruelty, ingratitude, and treachery, hath called his Maker's goodness in question, by puzzling us to account how a benevolent being should form so foolish and so vile an Animal" (bk. 8, chap. 15). The Man of the Hill has been persuaded to desert the world after a life in which his natural good instincts and animal spirits had been corrupted by his adventures in the world. The younger of two brothers, he received an education very different from that of his elder brother. Tom is in this way made aware of contrasting ways of life that are relevant to his own experiences in observing the lives of Western and Allworthy. The elder brother, somewhat the favorite of his mother, early devoted his life to the pleasures of the country and became an expert huntsman. The younger brother was set to books and in time found himself at Exeter College, Oxford, where he met two individuals who introduced him to two different types of urban corruption, which on the one hand, enticed him to maintain an appearance greater than his means allowed, and, on the other, led him to the hazards of the gaming table.

The first of these acquaintances was Sir George Gresham, who introduced the Man of the Hill to an expensive way of life which he could not afford, with the result that he stole from one of his fellow students and was forced to leave the university. Traveling up to London, he met a former collegian, one Watson, who introduced him to the varying fortunes of gambling. After some time passed, he had an opportunity to rescue a man who had been beaten by robbers, only to discover him to be his father.

Taking advantage of this chance occurrence, he returned home and devoted himself to serious study of both the classical authors and Scripture.
He now approached his studies more philosophically than he had at
Oxford and gained from them a wisdom that shaped his view of life. At his
father's death, he settled with his brother for the paternal estate and
traveled throughout Europe where he found life everywhere the same:
"The same hypocrisy, the same fraud; in short, the same follies and vices,
dressed in different habits" (bk. 8, chap. 15). Returning from these
travels, he retired to the life of an eccentric recluse, in which state Tom and
Partridge find him.

Fielding uses the story of the Man of the Hill to reveal both the
emotional and intellectual state of Tom's mind. Occasional references to
love as the tale is related evoke reactions of agitation or embarrassment
from Tom. In the discussion of human nature that follows the relation of
the story, however, a surprising maturity in Tom is revealed, and his
understanding of the relationship between benevolence and conduct is
suggested. At this point Tom has every reason to despair and to be
unhappy and tentative about the future. He is aware, moreover, that his
misfortunes have been brought about by his own shortcomings, as well as
through the malevolence of Blifil. Unlike the Man of the Hill, he has not
rejected the company of other human beings, nor has he failed to recognize
the existence of goodness, benevolence, and joy in the complex of human
experience.

The misanthropy of the Man of the Hill has brought him to an
involuted view of life in which contemplation becomes, not a part of the
act of living, but a substitute for it. "What time can suffice," he observes
to Jones, "for the contemplation and worship of that glorious, immortal,
and eternal Being. . . . Shall the trifling amusements, the palling pleasures, the silly business of the world, roll away our hours too swiftly from
us; and shall the pace of time seem sluggish to a mind exercised in studies
so high, so important, and so glorious!" (bk. 8, chap. 15).

Tom's response defines not only his view of mankind, but also the basic
ingredients that constitute his character. Although a young man, possessed not only of benevolence and natural goodness, but of animal spirits
and a love of life, he is neither passive nor naive in his assessment of
existence. He has observed mankind, but has seen the good along with the
bad. He cautions the Man of the Hill that he has made the common error of
judging by the worst of men, rather than by the best, and he significantly
reveals his reading of Shaftesbury when he notes that "an excellent writer
observes, nothing should be esteemed as characteristical of a Species, but

what is to be found among the best and most perfect individuals of the species," adding that, although he has not lived long, he has "known men worthy of the highest friendship, and women of the highest love." He is, moreover, aware of a basic goodness in people, and that much wickedness "arrives by mere accident, and many a man who commits evil, is not totally bad and corrupt in his heart" (bk. 8, chap. 15). Although this may sound like an apologia for Tom's conduct, it is much less that than a sincere and benevolent evaluation of the conduct of others, whose actions toward him might have embittered a less balanced person. For all his mature philosophy, however, Tom is still a man of the flesh, and his rescue of Mrs. Waters from the assault of Ensign Northerton that follows shortly upon this exchange with the Man of the Hill, arouses those sexual instincts that had led to his involvement with the daughter of Black George. Despite the fact that she is neither young nor beautiful, the fact that her clothes had been torn from the upper part of her body attracts his eyes to her breasts, "which were well formed, and extremely white," and he stares at them for some moments before turning his attention to the subdued Northerton (bk. 9, chap. 2). Tom then accompanies her to the inn at Upton where he sleeps with her.

Sophia herself listens to a parallel digressive tale, that told by Mrs. Fitzpatrick. Her narrative has a closer connection with the main story of the novel than does that of the Man of the Hill. She is personally a factor in the plot, for she conspires with Lady Bellaston to keep Sophia from Jones and, through Tom's duel with her husband, is responsible for the young man's imprisonment. In terms of the evolving characterization of Sophia, Mrs. Fitzpatrick's story, which is told on the way to London, has an effect similar to that which the adventures of the Man of the Hill has on Jones. Sophia, like Tom, is in a state of great personal turmoil and uncertainty, if not despair. She is fleeing a distasteful match with Blifil, which her father is determined to force upon her. The squire is following, and she must find means to escape his wrath. Finally, she has reason to question Tom's faithfulness to her. Although she loves Tom, the kind of husband he will make is a question she must resolve.

Sophia is, throughout the conversation, intensely interested in the details of Mrs. Fitzpatrick's story as well as in its final outcome. This may be attributed partly to her interest in romance, and partly to her sentimental concern for her cousin's unhappy situation. In addition, behind most of her reaction is her recognition of parallels between her own situation and that of Mrs. Fitzpatrick. There is an irregularity inherent in her proposed match with Tom that is perhaps greater than the fact of Mrs.

Fitzpatrick's marrying an Irishman, for Tom's true parents are unknown, and despite his charm and handsome appearance, he has already manifested a flaccidity of sexual disposition in his associations with Molly Seagrim and Mrs. Waters. He has, on the other hand, given evidence of charity, concern, and good sense; and so, at the end of Mrs. Fitzpatrick's tale of misery with her Irish husband, Sophia finds some consolation in her distant relation's observation on the causes of happiness or unhappiness in marriage. Rejecting Sophia's suggestion that she was at fault for marrying an Irishman, she defends many of that nationality: "There are, among the Irish, men of as much worth and honour as any among the English: nay, to speak the truth, generosity of spirit is rather more common among them. . . . Ask me, rather, what I could expect when I married a fool." To this Sophia timidly asks whether a man who is not a fool can make a bad husband, and, although Mrs. Fitzpatrick's answer contains some qualification, it must have been reassuring if not hopeful to Sophia, who had ample evidence that Jones was no fool. "Among my acquaintance," her cousin suggests, "the silliest fellows are the worst husbands; and I will venture to assert, as a fact, that a man of sense rarely behaves very ill to a wife, who deserves very well" (bk. 11, chap. 7). Sophia finds hope in Mrs. Fitzpatrick's tale of unhappiness in marriage because the conditions of her proposed union differ materially from Mrs. Fitzpatrick's experience, just as Tom finds in the story of the Man of the Hill reason not to join his host in hating mankind, but to affirm his own conviction that Shaftesbury is correct in asserting that the race should be judged by the best rather than the worst examples of it.

Fielding and the Sentimental Tradition

A proper reading of *Tom Jones* requires an understanding of the sentimental tradition in the theater and how it was manifested in fiction. The comedy of sensibility emerged in the theater after the turn of the eighteenth century and experienced its classic expression in the comedies of Richard Steele. His *Conscious Lovers,* an early illustration of the tradition, differs markedly from Richard Cumberland's *West Indian,* produced late in the century. While both aspects of the tradition idealize the middle class and find their heroes among either successful merchants or honest squires, there is a substantial difference in the social force that motivates them, the earlier tradition setting the outcome of love in marriage as paramount to its intention, the latter establishing charity and honesty toward one's neighbor as its central focus. The main thrust of Steele's play, for example, is the bringing together of Bevil, Jr., and Indiana in a happy marriage, departing significantly from the cynicism of Restoration attitudes toward love, while Cumberland focuses on the natural goodness, honesty, and charity of Belcour.

Among the novelists, the earlier attitude is reflected in Richardson's idealization of marriage as the object of love in his three great novels, *Pamela, Clarissa,* and *Charles Grandison.* The moral structure of life is centered on marriage and adjustments to the social problems that stand in the way of achieving happiness in that state. In the novels a more cynical than ideal view of love is expressed by Mr. B-- in *Pamela,* by Lovelace in *Clarissa,* and by Hargrave Polexfen in *Grandison,* with Sir Charles in the last novel functioning as a contrasting ideal. Fielding, while moving his characters toward success in marriage, is much less concerned with sexual mores and morality than he is with moral goodness as it is expressed through charity. The earlier sentimental tradition has little or nothing to do with charity and the human relationships that are dependent on it, but concentrates on the gamesmanship of love and eventual marriage. The later tradition, developed in the novel by Fielding and in the drama by Cumberland, derives significantly from that optimistic attitude toward human nature that is characteristic of Shaftesbury.

While retaining the middle-class orientation of sentiment and still holding out the ideal of marriage as the outgrowth of love, Fielding adheres to a relative scale of ethical values, seeing the relationship of man to man in terms of his commitment to assist those in need as more significant than sexual purity. For this reason, Fielding's heroes are basically good, though perhaps flawed in an aspect of moral virtue that is less significant than charity. As in *A Journey from this World to the Next,* Fielding demands positive indications of benevolence toward one's fellow creatures. This test is met by the male protagonists of all his novels, by Joseph Andrews and Tom Jones, as well as by Heartfree in *Jonathan Wild* and Captain Booth in *Amelia.* Tom's conduct differs significantly from that of Joseph, in his being possessed of substantial faults that cause Sophia great pain, but that, in his flaccid, amoral attitude toward sex, he is unable to perceive. Joseph Andrews possesses no major faults and, largely for this reason, is unable to capture the imagination of the reader as consistently as does Tom Jones.

Tom's failure to perceive the likely consequences of his sexual encounters results largely from ebullient natural spirits that prompt him to live life to the full and that place little check on his natural appetites. He is, to be sure, not naive and has had considerable experience in life by viewing the contrasting households of Allworthy and Western. For twenty years he has witnessed the activities of life in neighboring villages, and he has been

treated to a reasonable amount of educative training at the hands of
Thwackum and Square, whose instruction has insisted on surface morality
and appearances, rather than basic good nature. His tutors represent
values, on the one hand rigidly religious, on the other deistic, that run
counter to Tom's general sense of good nature and charity. Strictures about
sex seem artificially rigid to Tom, who appears to have little inclination
toward formal religion. Certainly they are not strong enough to counter
the pressing temptations of animal spirits, inflamed by alcohol and the
willing and anxious availability of Molly Seagrim. Ebullient natural
instincts dominate Tom's actions, which are made to appear less offensive
than the acts of deceit and malice of Blifil, who is generally praised by his
pedagogues. Balance in the characterization of Tom is achieved by Fielding's emphasis on how his natural instincts also result in generosity and
charity.

In Fielding's last novel, *Amelia,* he examines sexual infidelity in married
life and provides an examination of moral flaccidity in Captain Booth that
seems to represent a third stage in the study of a significant moral
dilemma. The first two novels, *Joseph Andrews* and *Jonathan Wild,* consider
sexual morality in premarital life and in married life respectively. In each
instance, both hero and heroine are beyond reproach, and no scale of
relative values is established to judge the conduct of either Joseph and
Fanny, on the one hand, or of Heartfree and his wife on the other.
Although charity is a major factor in both novels, it does not rival chastity
as a virtue and neither hero nor heroine possesses one without the other. In
Fielding's last two novels the issues of charity and of love are no longer
discrete ones, and both Jones and Booth are men of goodwill and benevolent heart, but flawed by weaknesses related to their capacity to meet the
obligations of love and marriage normally imposed by society. Tom's
sexual indiscretions come to an end with his marriage to Sophia, but
Captain Booth's only begin with marriage. As will appear from the
subsequent discussion of *Amelia,* Booth's conversion is the result of
religious influences. In Tom's case it is the result of the sentimental
recognition of the virtue and beauty of Sophia.

Fielding's Characterization

Most of Fielding's characters contain a mixture of good and bad qualities, and only rarely does the malevolent disposition of an individual
govern his actions. One such person emerges, however, in each novel: Lady
Booby in *Joseph Andrews,* Wild himself in *Jonathan Wild,* Blifil in *Tom*

Jones, and Captain Trent in *Amelia.* Blifil is the one genuinely evil person in *Tom Jones,* and his character is unrelieved either by compensating virtues or by human suffering that might have mitigated his conduct. While many characters in Fielding's novels are guilty of altering appearances to present themselves in a more favorable light, Blifil is a devoted hypocrite, whose actions are designed to destroy his rival, Tom. Tom, on the other hand, sincerely loves Blifil and, on occasion, makes him his confidant. Blifil uses this to his advantage, for instance, when Tom is caught pursuing a partridge into a neighbor's estate while hunting with Black George. Unwilling to reveal the name of the gamekeeper, who had with some reluctance accompanied him, Tom fully accepts the blame and is severely whipped. Unfortunately, he confides the truth to Blifil, who waits for an opportunity to reveal the identity of Black George when the two boys quarrel over Blifil's calling Tom a "beggarly Bastard." The incident serves not only to reveal the true generosity and natural kindness of Tom, but also the jealous, malicious nature of Blifil, who, without lying directly, uses the truth to make Tom appear in as bad a light as possible.

Both Thwackum and Square applaud Blifil's conduct on this occasion, but Allworthy recognizes much to commend in Tom's generous effort to protect his friend, Black George. Allworthy's understanding of Tom's action, however, does not save George from the wrath of the squire, who dismisses the gamekeeper for not admitting his guilt and for allowing Tom to bear the full punishment. The scene serves to prepare the reader for the more damaging event in which Blifil, again for the most malicious of motives, distorts the appearance of Tom's actions following Allworthy's illness, to make him seem guilty of extreme ingratitude.

In these actions Blifil follows the malevolent type of motivation often found in dramas and novels of sentiment. In George Lillo's *London Merchant* Millwood plots and brings about the complete destruction of Barnwell because of a pathological hatred of men; in *Jonathan Wild* the master criminal pursues Heartfree because he hates the merchant for having befriended him. Similarly, Blifil has a distorted psyche that cannot endure the youthful goodness of Tom, whose affection intensifies Blifil's jealous spirit that brings into focus his vicious desire to destroy his companion and rival. Lady Bellaston functions as a second villain, but with more understandably selfish motives, as she attempts to prevent the marriage of Tom and Sophia. Her efforts to have Lord Fellamar engage the affections of Sophia echo Lady Booby's desire to have Beau Didapper wed Fanny in *Joseph Andrews.* In each instance, efforts to thwart the normal outcome of love in the young couple reflect a psychologically disturbed personality that pursues a vengeful objective with surprising intensity.

The one dominant passion that seems to rule most of the characters in Fielding's novels is generally leavened by human shortcomings from which they suffer. Allworthy is as close to perfection as any novelist dealing with a valid picture of humanity can draw him, but even in him peccadillos may be recognized. Allworthy suffers from a credulity that flaws his claim to perfection and results in his participating unwittingly in substantial injustice. Thwackum and Square, on whom must fall much of the responsibility for the training of Blifil and Jones, and whose actions contribute to the misfortunes of the hero, are not vicious individuals but materialistically narrow and distorted in their views. Had they been evil men, or possessed of more than the ordinary faults of men in the world, Allworthy would have undoubtedly dismissed them from his service. Their actions grow out of ideas that are common in the society in which they live. Square develops a great hatred for Tom Jones, born of jealousy over Mrs. Blifil's affection for Tom when he grew to manhood. Although Mrs. Blifil had been critical of Tom in the early years of his life, obviously as a means of masking the fact that she was his mother, as he grew older she saw in him much to admire, and her affection for him seemed to outweigh that which she had for her known son, Blifil. This maternal affection is mistaken for erotic love by Square, with whom it was rumored Tom's mother had long been romantically involved.

An incident that occurs at this time in Tom's life provides an early indication of his charitable nature and demonstrates how differently Thwackum and Square act toward Tom as opposed to Blifil. In order to relieve the distresses of Black George and his family after the gamekeeper has been dismissed, Tom sells a horse given him by the squire. Thwackum is indignant, but Allworthy forgiving on this occasion. For the same reason, Tom also sells a Bible given to him by the squire, this time to Blifil, who deliberately makes a fetish of reading the Bible in public for the vicious purpose of revealing the fact that Tom has sold it. Blifil's malevolent conduct, in betraying Tom's trust while fully aware of Tom's charitable motives, is characteristic of his actions throughout the novel. There is little that can be offered to redeem his character on any occasion. Thwackum, on the other hand, finds pious reasons for criticizing Tom, arguing that selling a Bible is sacrilegious and must be punished. Square takes a contrary position, much to the disgust of Thwackum, not out of any appreciation of Tom's actions, but because his rational ethic sees no difference between selling one book or another.

The actions of Blifil, Thwackum, and Square at the time Tom is exiled by Allworthy provide crucial evidence of their characters. Fielding has carefully prepared for Tom's departure, by not only explaining the reasons for Allworthy's behavior but by showing the motivations for the actions of Blifil and Thwackum that lead to it. Only Allworthy's firm conviction that Tom is guilty of ingratitude could have justified sending him away, and he comes to this judgment on the distorted testimony of Blifil and Thwackum. The event grows out of Allworthy's illness and the apparent, imminent danger of his death. The scene reveals the attitudes of the principal characters toward Allworthy, as each reacts to the announcement of the provisions of his will. Blifil is made his principal heir and granted his entire estate, with the exception of several specific bequests. Chief among these is that to Tom of five hundred pounds a year plus ready cash in the amount of one thousand pounds. Thwackum and Square each receive a thousand-pound bequest, and an additional three thousand pounds is allocated in smaller gifts to the servants and to Allworthy's favorite charities. The reactions of all but Tom suggest little affection for the squire, and Blifil gives evidence of a desire to hasten his death.

Tom's reaction demonstrates real concern for the squire. He is grateful to him for his generosity, but his chief emotion is distress at his impending death. Thwackum and Square are both dissatisfied with their portion of the inheritance, Thwackum, who consistently works in close harmony with Blifil, being more vocally critical of Allworthy. Thwackum complains of Allworthy's not observing the formalities of religion, since he has not asked him to hear his confession as death approaches. Blifil's reaction is characteristic. He gives himself to exaggerated expressions of mourning, obviously designed to impress not only Allworthy, but also Thwackum. More significant is his response to his own mother's death, and his decision whether or not to tell Allworthy about it. Despite the physician's contrary advice, he insists on making the revelation. Under the circumstances, it is clear that he passes on the bad news with the hope that it will hasten the squire's death and bring him to the immediate possession of the estate.

Once Allworthy recovers, Blifil acts to lay the groundwork for denying Tom the inheritance intended for him. He continues the efforts to cast an unfavorable light on Tom's actions. He finds an opportunity to quarrel with Tom over his supposed failure to show proper respect for Mrs. Blifil's death, and he provocatively insults Tom over his illegitimate birth. The physical altercation that follows is quickly brought to a close by neutral parties, but it prepares for the more serious fight that follows Blifil and Thwackum's discovery of Tom with Molly, in which both Blifil and his companion are seriously beaten. The intensity of the anger and resentment of both Blifil and Thwackum heightens their malicious distortion of Tom's motives. Blifil is acutely conscious of Tom as a rival for Allworthy's estate, for he has been given a letter from his mother for delivery to Allworthy, revealing that she is also Tom's mother. Blifil keeps this secret, while revealing the news of his mother's death. While this fact is withheld from the reader until the closing pages of the novel, it explains in retrospect much of Blifil's motivation. Viciously moving to turn Allworthy against Tom, he succeeds temporarily, revealing the unrelieved and unmitigated evil of his character. The reversal of Blifil's fortune at the conclusion leaves the reader with no sense of pity for him when he is rejected by Allworthy.

Thwackum has much less to gain than Blifil, and his nature is not marked by malevolent hatred. For him, Tom is a recalcitrant pupil whom he cannot bring to heel. His resentment is not viciously motivated, and to some extent it is dictated by an exaggerated sense of religion that he professes with at least some degree of sincerity. Thwackum, moreover, has another role to play in helping to establish, from a negative point of view, Tom's attitude toward formal religion, just as Square is important in making it clear that Tom does not embrace a deistic view of existence. As the complex motivations that govern the actions of Blifil and Thwackum create a situation in which Tom must confront the realities of physical survival in the world, they also force him into circumstances in which he cannot avoid a personal assessment of life and its ethical and moral implications.

Tom's exile has its impact on Sophia, who is also thrust into the world and forced to adopt attitudes toward marriage and family life at an accelerated pace. Her education for life had begun with her experiencing the crude habits of Squire Western. She is given an emotional jolt and taught an important lesson in how to survive when she discovers Tom's indiscrete involvement with Molly Seagrim and must react to it. She learns of his physical if not romantic connection with another woman, just as he comes to grasp the reality of his affection for her and her reciprocation of it. In this sense, the affairs surrounding Allworthy's illness, and the activities they trigger, admirably set the stage for the journeys both Tom and Sophia make to London.

The Prefatory Chapters

The prefatory chapters to each of the books of *Tom Jones* form a conscious and important part of Fielding's design for the novel. In the introduction to book 16, the novelist comments on the reason for the introductory chapters, specifically indicating the difficulties faced in their composition, comparing it to the task of providing prologues in the theater. Noting that he can "with less pains write one of the books of this history than the prefatory chapter to each of them," he adds that most such chapters, "like modern prologues, may as properly be prefixed to any other book in this history as to that which they introduce, or indeed to any other history as to this." While this may be true of many individual chapters, the order in which they are presented does in fact contribute to the ability of the reader to understand the theory behind Fielding's fiction. It allows the author, moreover, to explain specific parts of the background and to prepare for the entrance of key characters, such as that of Sophia in book 4.

In general, three substantive areas are explored in the various introductory sections: first, the theory of the new form of the "heroic, historical, prosaic poem" that Fielding is attempting to write; second, the relationship of the critic to the author with observations on the obligations of the critic; and third, the exploration of several philosophical themes on which the meaning of the work turns.

The theory of the novel developed in *Tom Jones* is an extension of that advanced in the introduction to *Joseph Andrews*. Fielding seems more aware, however, of the relationship that exists between the writer and the reader, not merely in the sense that the reader must be pleased and entertained, but in the more profound realization of how this particular type of fiction works on the reader's sensibility. The nature of comedy requires both a body of knowledge shared by reader and writer and the existence of reader experience, of which the writer can take advantage. The introductory chapters provide Fielding with an opportunity to break down the differences in perspective that may exist between himself and the reader, and to draw the reader into an intimacy with him that results in a seeming friendship and rapport. Much, therefore, can be inferred rather than spoken, and ideas can be introduced into the complex of the reader's experience. In this way, the more serious purpose of the novelist, his ability to influence the moral perspective of the reader, is significantly advanced.

Much that Fielding says about his fiction was commonplace in the eighteenth century. It is not surprising that he should call nature the source of his work, nor that he should emphasize the entertainment feature of fiction. What is more important, he capitalizes on the uniformity of human nature, demonstrating how it operates in both rural and urban settings (bk. 1, chap. 1). Fielding manages to transcend the particular historical time in which the novel is set to focus on the more important factors of human existence that are centered in the struggle of each human being to understand the appropriate role he should pursue in life. He sheds light on the relationship between action that is perceived and motivation that is often hidden, noting how significant this is in judging the conduct of individuals. It is a theme that Fielding consistently advances, emphasizing the disparity between substance and appearance, between what men say and what they mean, and between the natural instincts of humanity and the pressures brought upon those instincts by civilization. By having both Tom and Sophia travel from the country to the city, he portrays them first in the natural environment of rural life, a life not without its vices and its moral shortcomings, but a life in which human action is less touched by the trappings of civilization than in the complex structure of London.

The sources of human action and the causes of human evil operate in both locales with equal intensity, however. The viciousness of Blifil and the weakness of Thwackum and Square are as apparent in the country as the vices of Lady Bellaston and the entrepreneurs of high life are in London. Ultimately, the reader learns that happiness as well as moral guilt or innocence rests in the individual himself, and not in the artificialities of circumstance. Tom, in the midst of all his distresses, has a more morally valid perspective than the Man of the Hill despite all of the latter's experience in the world; and Sophia's natural goodness enables her to make a more mature judgment of Tom than Mrs. Fitzpatrick's distorted sense of reality allows her to make about life. Moreover, the city is not the province of the rich and dissolute alone; and the good and the poor, the Millers and the Nightingales, as well as the Lady Bellastons and the Lord Fellamars inhabit it. Affectation and vice emerge as the common inheritance of mankind whatever the geographic or social setting in which the individual lives. In a large measure, Fielding uses his introductory sections to develop a sophisticated rapport with his reader that enables this fundamental idea to be grasped and accepted as an essential truth on which much of the irony of the novel is developed.

Fielding's discussion of the critic and his role focuses on significant aspects of reading often disregarded by critics whose emphasis is merely on finding faults in works examined. Such critics often see shortcomings in a work because they themselves have not understood it. In the introductory chapter to book 10 Fielding notes how the editors of Shakespeare have often misunderstood or misrepresented him because they have not recognized his real intentions in a work. The result is that the ordinary reader is often led to an erroneous reading by the critic. Fielding seeks, by the obvious comparison of critical treatment of Shakespeare with the expected treatment of his own work, to blunt the effect of erroneous readings by malicious critics.

Moreover, he brings directly to the reader matters essential to the full understanding of the novel and to a proper evaluation of the chief characters in it, especially Tom Jones himself.

In reading *Tom Jones*, the reader must understand how Fielding tends to link character with individual traits of personality, rather than to attitudes attributable to the particular walk of life to which a person is called. The discriminations that separate one member of a class from another become significant, as may be recognized in the portraits of the two squires, Allworthy and Western. Both men are essentially good, but each represents a different cultural and social view of life, and it would be erroneous to see in their occupations a basis for characterizing them. Circumstances of birth often weigh heavily in the public mind, and the character of the illegitimate child is frequently interpreted in the light of the circumstances of his birth. Tom suffers from this and is automatically judged to have a bad nature and a bad character, so that actions that are merely the result of the wildness of youth are seen in darker colors than they might be in the case of an ordinary young man. Even Allworthy is ready to condemn Tom when he banishes him, perhaps subtly influenced by the knowledge of his origin.

While ostensibly speaking to the critic, Fielding seems to address his reader directly when he observes: ". . . we must admonish thee . . . not to condemn a character as a bad one, because it is not perfectly a good one. If thou dost delight in these models of perfection, there are books enow written to gratify thy taste; but, as we have not, in the course of our conversation, ever happened to meet with any such person, we have not chosen to introduce any such here" (bk. 10, chap. 1). Ultimately, what is important is Fielding's direct appeal to the reader to disregard the censures of the critic, for the critic can mislead through ignorance as well as malice, by commenting on a work without having read it and by condemning the whole without having perceived the individual parts and their interrelationship. The reader is thus invited to become his own critic and to trust his own reactions as he pursues the discovery of truth through the medium of fiction.

Fielding introduces a number of philosophical themes that he wishes the reader to be aware of, not the least of which are the nature of truth and the nature of love. Modern readings of the novel suggest that the nature of prudence is central to Fielding's message. Prudence, of course, involves choice, and choice is made possible only by the knowledge of alternatives. Joseph Andrews has little area of choice, for he has a monochromatic ethical view of life. Early brought under the influence of Parson Adams, there is little that he can be tempted to do that would divert him from the path of virtue, and his pursuit of Fanny involves merely overcoming the difficulties the ordinary man faces in life, and he does not confront any serious moral dilemma. By the same token, Heartfree has a clear pattern for his conduct and relentlessly pursues it. In *Tom Jones* and *Amelia,* however, the pattern of choice is significant, and the formation of the moral character of the hero is the central means by which the reader is led to benefit from Fielding's insight. Understanding the nature of moral choice and the dimension of the moral dilemma that often results from its confrontation, requires a perception of issues such as the nature of truth and love.

Fielding relates the world's understanding of love to the more general tendency to confuse appearance and reality. Of all the distortions of reality caused by vanity and hypocrisy, and the misconceptions by which the world judges the conduct of the individual, the way in which the word "love" is twisted out of shape is perhaps the most destructive. Crucial to the understanding of Tom Jones is a perception of what the word "love" means to him, to those with whom he associates, and to the reader. The introductory section to book 6 is Fielding's attempt to share with the reader his sense of how love, whether seen as charity or lust, should be understood.

The discussion begins by linking the attitudes of those who would deny the existence of love with the same philosophical temperament that Swift habitually attacks, that of the tampering experimenter. The same pride that leads the philosophical experimenter to conclude that there is no God, or that human nature lacks virtue or goodness, will inevitably deny the existence of the passion of love. In a scathing passage Fielding attacks the "truth finder": "Whereas the truth-finder, having raked out that jakes, his own mind, and being there capable of tracing no ray of divinity, nor anything virtuous, or good, or lovely, or loving, very fairly, honestly, and logically concludes that no such things exist in the whole Creation." Fielding distinguishes the animal appetite, more commonly called lust, from real love, which is a "kind and benevolent disposition which is gratified by contributing to the happiness of others" (bk. 6, chap. 1). Most important in understanding *Tom Jones* is the nature of true and benevolent love, that seeks its satisfaction with as much intensity as that of the grossest of appetites, although it does so "in a much more delicate manner." Moreover, when the passion of true love is directed toward the opposite sex, it finds its strongest outlet in physical love, and the combination of the spiritual and the physical "heightens all its delights to a degree scarce imaginable by those who have never been susceptible of any other emotions than what have proceeded from appetite alone" (bk. 6, chap. 1).

Tom's relationship with Molly Seagrim or with Mrs. Waters would not meet Fielding's definition of true love. Physical love alone is the essential ingredient of those holidays from virtue, whereas the relationship that Tom has with Sophia springs from a different source. Fielding identifies "esteem and gratitude" with "love," and "youth and beauty" with desire, but the two, when combined in the sensibilities of a benevolent man and a virtuous woman, produce a profound and lasting effect. Even the ravages of age and sickness "can have no effect on love, nor ever shake or remove, from a good mind, that sensation or passion which hath gratitude and esteem for its basis." This concept is an essential thesis of the novel, which can be seen as a moving panegyric on love. "If you do not" grasp this, Fielding tells his reader, "you have already read more than you have understood" (bk. 6, chap. 1).

Love is not merely exemplified in the ideal relationship that exists between Tom and Sophia, but equally in the benevolence of Allworthy, who exudes concern for others and endeavors to bring happiness to the deserving. The expression of Allworthy's love is limited by his responsibility for governing both his family and those who live on or near his land. He must combine judgment with concern and punish or reward those with whom he has contact. There is never any doubt that he is a good and benevolent individual, but his ability to bring happiness to others is at times diminished by the weakness of his perceptions. For Tom, on the other hand, whose naturally benevolent instincts find expression in a love for Sophia that begins with the highest esteem and is nurtured by romantic and physical attraction, there is no limit to its expression or to the happiness it can bring. The initial flaccidity of Tom's amorous actions gives way to the solidity of love, and there is no danger of a relapse, both because of his esteem for Sophia and his gratitude for the way she has understood his shortcomings.

Square, who undergoes a conversion to true Christianity, establishes a link between benevolence and religion. The "pride of philosophy" had "intoxicated" his reason (bk. 18, chap. 4), but his newly found true understanding of Christianity permits him to recognize the importance of gratitude and the value of Tom's adherence to duty. For this reason, he informs Allworthy about the young man's fidelity to both of these virtues. The novel thus pivots on love, properly understood, and establishes the place of benevolence in the relationship that should exist between man and man, and man and his creator.

Tom Jones has deservedly been recognized as Fielding's masterpiece, with critics seeking to explain its quality in many ways. The plot structure of the novel, intricate and complex, is brilliantly executed, relating even seemingly minute events that occur early in the novel to its final outcome. Although not discovered by the reader until near the end of the novel, the revelation of Blifil's true nature by the simplest of deceits, the withholding from Allworthy the contents of his mother's letter about Tom's birth, is highly appropriate for it adds base dishonesty to malice and reveals how that which is often unnoticed is highly indicative of the reality that lies behind deceit.

What seems to be a superficial trick of the plot to extricate the novelist from the complex web that he has created is in reality a master stroke that links the beginning and end of the novel to reveal the overwhelming ironic vision through which the novelist observes life. Blifil's character fades into incalculably dark shadows, as an incident so small that it might almost never have occurred comes to light and is recognized as having set in motion most of the main action of the novel. In this way *Tom Jones* becomes a study of evil and the ethical dilemmas that confront the good man as he strives to find a rationale for living. *Tom Jones,* the product of Fielding's aesthetic vision, takes its place among the literary masterpieces of Swift and Pope in studying the impact of pride and ambition on man's ethical conduct.

Chapter Five

Final Achievement in Fiction: *Amelia*

In December, 1751, Fielding published his last novel, *Amelia*, a book obscured by the shadow of *Tom Jones*, but in its own right one of the fine fictional productions of the eighteenth century. In its treatment of married life *Amelia* bears a relationship to *Tom Jones* that parallels that of *Jonathan Wild* to *Joseph Andrews*. The Heartfree episode of the *Wild* story presents, in a highly sentimental vein, the problems faced by two basically good married people in meeting the difficulties life imposes as honesty comes into confrontation with dishonesty, and connubial virtue into conflict with the predatory instincts of the master criminal. This balances in married life the story of Joseph Andrews and Fanny, whose tale concerns their adventures prior to the sanctification of their love in marriage. In *Tom Jones* Fielding again treats of unmarried love, but in a less sentimental and more realistic framework than he had in *Joseph Andrews*. Both Tom and Sophia possess more of the frailties of human nature than do their counterparts in *Joseph Andrews,* and their path to happiness confronts to a greater extent the harsh realities of both rural and urban life in eighteenth-century England. While the tale of Tom and Sophia concentrates on the developing maturity of Tom and his preparation for married life with Sophia, *Amelia* focuses on the impact that an unsettled vision of life has on the continuing happiness of two married people, Captain Booth and Amelia. The protagonists of Fielding's last novel find their bliss threatened by the pressures of civilization, generated partly by the world outside them, but to a large extent by Booth's incapacity to meet with resolution the inevitable struggles of life.

Fielding sets the novel in London during the spring of an unspecified year in which William Booth, an officer in the British army, has been wounded twice at the siege of Gibraltar, but, because of a reduction in the size of his regiment, has been retired on half pay. He is imprisoned because he imprudently goes to the defense of a man being beaten by two others and is himself seized as the aggressor. Seven years before this event, he had married Amelia, a beautiful and faithful young woman of admirable virtue and devotion. Although a young man of naturally good instincts, Booth suffers from an inability to come to grips with life. With the help of a generous clergyman, Dr. Harrison, he attempted to establish a small farm, but, when a combination of vanity and ineptitude caused the venture to fail, he and Amelia, with two of their children, fled to London to avoid imprisonment for debt. They took up quarters in the verge of the court, the area of London where debtors were protected from arrest.

Booth finds himself in prison with two individuals who will alter the course of his life, a former acquaintance, Miss Matthews, and a gambler named Robinson. For some time Fanny Matthews has had amorous designs on Booth, and, presently in affluent circumstances, she is able to purchase a private apartment in the prison to which she has been confined for stabbing her lover. She persuades Booth to share her quarters, and, despite his genuine love for Amelia, his pliant disposition allows him to enter into a temporary sexual relationship with her. When it is finally learned that the man injured by Miss Matthews will survive, she is released from prison and purchases Booth's freedom.

Amelia and her two older children now appear, as Booth joins her at the modest rooms they have rented from Mrs. Ellison, who seems to be the friendly proprietress of a rooming house but who functions as the bawd of a disreputable peer in trapping young married women into sexual entanglements. With the aid of Mrs. Ellison, the peer tries to seduce Amelia by feigning concern for her husband's future and by giving expensive gifts to her children. Fortunately for Amelia, she meets a former victim of the peer, Mrs. Bennet, who warns her just before the final seduction attempt is to be made.

Booth, meanwhile, meets an old friend with whom he served at Gibraltar, Colonel James, and, distraught over his brief affair with Miss Matthews, confides the matter to him. This is a mistake, for James has been supplying Miss Matthews with money in the hope of securing her as a mistress. The colonel visits Booth, meets Amelia, and falls in love with her. When Booth is trapped into leaving the verge of the court and is arrested and imprisoned for debt, Colonel James attempts to keep him there while he tries to seduce Amelia, but Booth is saved by the arrival of Dr. Harrison, who arranges for his release. Mrs. Bennet has privately married Sergeant Atkinson, another acquaintance of Booth, and when she learns that Colonel James has invited Amelia and Booth to accompany his party to a masquerade, and that Amelia desires not to go, she arranges to go in her place. This causes complications for Amelia, for it indirectly encourages the dissolute peer. Mrs. Bennet, in the guise of Amelia, meets the nobleman and tries to advance the cause of her husband in obtaining a commission. Naturally, the peer expects a return for the favor which he believes he has bestowed on Amelia, rather than on Mrs. Bennet.

With his mind still on Amelia, the peer engages another former friend of Booth, Captain Trent, to draw Booth into a game of cards with sharpers, to lend him money when he loses, and thus to so involve him in debt that he can use the threat of debtors' prison to persuade Amelia to yield to his advances. Although Amelia attempts to help her husband by selling all her possessions and giving him the money to pay his debt to Trent, Booth, with characteristic imprudence, uses the money to bribe an employee in the war office to obtain a commission for him. As might be expected, this attempt fails. In the interim, Miss Matthews compels Booth to visit her in her apartment under the threat of revealing to Amelia their former relationship in prison. Finally, Booth is arrested and imprisoned for debt.

Amelia, attempting to cheer her husband, prepares a small supper for him, only to find that he does not return. Instead, she intercepts a message from the jealous Colonel James, challenging Booth to a duel because of his visit to Miss Matthews. Amelia's unhappiness reaches a low point as her learning of Booth's visit to Miss Matthews is followed by news of his imprisonment. From these depths, circumstances begin to improve. Dr. Harrison persuades Colonel James to drop his challenge to Booth, and Robinson, who had appeared earlier as one of Booth's fellow inmates during his first imprisonment, reveals that Amelia's mother had written a will leaving the bulk of her substantial estate to Amelia. He also tells how, in Amelia's absence at Gibraltar to be with Booth, a dishonest attorney, in collusion with her sister, forged the will that had disinherited Amelia. At this point, the couple's financial future is assured, but Booth's amoral view of life remains a barrier to their happiness. While in prison, however, Booth reads the sermons of Dr. Barrow and is converted to a firm view of Christianity that leads the reader to believe that he is prepared to undertake the responsibilities of married life, and that all will now be well between him and the forgiving Amelia. They leave London for the country, where their family grows to include six children, and they are blessed with great domestic happiness.

Amelia as a Sociological Document

Amelia is a thoughtful book that crystallizes Fielding's social views and relates the individual's ability to confront life to his religious sensibilities. The book explores through fiction questions of crime, the law, and prison life, questions that had occupied Fielding's life as Justice of the Peace for Westminster, and that he had addressed in his *Enquiry into the Causes of the Late Increase of Robbers,* in *A Charge Delivered to the Grand Jury* (1749), and in his *Proposal for Making an Effectual Provision for the Poor.* He returns, moreover, to the themes concerning charity that he had treated in both the *Champion* and the *Covent Garden Journal.* Importantly, he advances a theory about life that places the responsibility for the fate of the individual not on the idiosyncrasies of fate but on causes traceable to himself and the actions of others. The difficulties men experience, he suggests, are traceable to the immoderate and undisciplined pursuit of a predominant passion. "Life," Fielding tells the reader in the opening chapter of *Amelia,* "may as properly be called an art as any other; and the great incidents in it are no more to be considered as mere accidents than the several members of a fine statue or a noble poem." The novel clearly demonstrates how the common actions of men that result in the creation and enforcement of law, in the judicial system, and in methods of treating debtors are as important to the fate of the individual as are his own actions.

Fielding reveals significant shortcomings in the legal structure of English society in the eighteenth century, in the method of apprehending criminals, in the inadequate preparation and supervision of justices, and in the prison system.[1] In the novel Booth's unjust arrest and imprisonment illustrate how social prejudice, the inadequacy of the watch, and an irresponsible justice can bring an innocent man to undeserved incarceration. Moreover, the prison scene itself, illustrative of the unjust practice of garnish and the way crime itself maintains the prison system, provides moving portraits of individuals whose arrest is itself a criticism of society. Among the assortment of petty criminals, prostitutes, and thieves the prison also holds those whose only crime is being poor. A "young woman in rags sitting on the ground, and supporting the head of an old man in her lap, who appeared to be giving up the ghost," has been arrested because she has stolen a loaf of bread to support her father, and he, because he has accepted stolen property. Even more pathetic is the case of the poor soldier who has been wounded at Gibraltar and, after his discharge from the hospital, has been arrested for stealing herrings from a fishmonger. Though acquitted several months later, he has been kept in prison for the nonpayment of fees (bk. 1, chap. 4).

Amid fine realistic scenes and lively characterizations of prisoners, Booth's character evolves through both the revelation of his religious sensibilities and the compassion with which he views many of his fellow inmates. Booth's religious ideas are contrasted with those of his new acquaintance, Robinson, whom Fielding describes as "a freethinker—that is to say, a deist, or, perhaps, an atheist; for though he did not absolutely deny the existence of a God, yet he entirely denied his providence. A doctrine which, if it is not downright atheism, hath a direct tendency toward it; and as Dr. Clarke observes, may soon be driven into it" (bk. 1, chap. 3). Fielding treats freethinkers roughly in the periodicals, and, although Robinson has some compensating facets to his character, his moral attitudes are clearly condemned. They serve, moreover, to define those of Booth, who is wavering and uncertain in his idea of religion. The distinguishing difference between Booth and Robinson lies in the fact that Booth is a "well-wisher to religion," despite his "slight and uncertain" notions of it. Booth's view of providence is derived, unwisely, Fielding suggests, from his own misfortunes: "In short, poor Booth imagined that a larger share of misfortunes had fallen to his lot than he had merited; and this led him, who (though a good classical scholar) was not deeply learned in religious matters, into a disadvantageous opinion of Providence" (bk. 1, chap. 3). By introducing Robinson to Booth, Fielding introduces his theme of individual responsibility, for Robinson affirms that "all things happen by an inevitable finality," while Booth modifies this view to place the blame on man's acting "merely from the force of that passion which was uppermost in his mind," asserting that he "could do no otherwise" (bk. 1, chap. 3).

Booth illustrates one type of individual that Fielding presents as a worthy object of charity in the *Champion.* His being bred to life in the army has left him with no way of making a living outside that career, and he thus illustrates the sort of individual described in the *Champion* of February 16, 1739–40:

The first and chief objects of our charity are such persons as, having been educated in genteel life, with moderate fortunes, partly through want of resolution to quit the character in which they were bred, and partly for want of duly considering the consequences of their expenses, have, by following their superiors into luxury, in order to support, as they call it, the figure of gentlemen, reduced themselves to distress and poverty.

The story of Booth's life before the action of the novel begins is related in the form of a flashback reminiscent of epic poetry, and the parallel between *Amelia* and Vergil's *Aeneid* has long been noted.[2] The refuge in a cave sought by Dido and Aeneas while a storm rages outside is an appropriate model for the refuge that Booth seeks in the prison apartment of Miss Matthews, as a hostile world of prison life surrounds them. It is a loose parallel, more structural than substantive, but Aeneas's conflict with duty in his temporary relationship with Dido is brought to mind by the temporary love entanglement of Booth and Fanny Matthews. The reader must wait for Miss Matthews to tell the story of her unfortunate love and to explain her imprisonment for murder, before the unfortunate Booth can recount his tale of love and marriage to Amelia, to the ears of the unappreciative Miss Matthews. Her tawdry recitation contrasts with the idyllic story of the love that Amelia has bestowed on her errant husband. Both Booth's sentimental nature and his innate moral earnestness are revealed through his recitation to his prison companion. The reader learns how he warned Amelia that their marriage might be unwise because of his poverty and how Dr. Harrison, after learning of Booth's sincerity in trying to protect Amelia, became his staunch advocate and arranged for their marriage. Booth's sentimental nature caused him to rush spontaneously to the deathbed of his dying sister, but to leave her as impetuously when he learned that his marriage was threatened. Through actions such as these, Booth is characterized as a man with generous instincts, but of a highly emotional and impetuous nature. Such tendencies combine with his reasoned conviction that his actions, like those of all other men, are governed by those passions that dominate at a given moment. Lacking prudential control over actions that are not based on moral principles, Booth lives for the moment. This inconsistency of purpose makes plausible the deeply sentimental love that Booth has for Amelia, even while he lives in a temporary adulterous relationship with Miss Matthews.

Booth and Amelia might have lived in decent circumstances had he retained his commission in the army and had she received her expected inheritance from her mother, but such was not to be the case, as turns of fortune saw Booth retired on half pay and Amelia apparently disinherited. Even the interposing of Dr. Harrison failed, for the good man, after setting Booth and Amelia up as farmers by renting them his parsonage, was unable to remain and supervise their actions. The doctor's departure to become tutor to his patron's son left Booth without guidance, and he fell into many errors. He attempted to enlarge his farm by renting a neighboring one, and the enterprise failed. His uniting his family with that of the curate of the parish led to both personal and financial difficulties. The greatest of all his mistakes, however, was to arouse the envy of his neighbors by the purchase of an old coach and harness in order to fulfill a lifelong ambition to own a coach. Prompted by envy, his neighbors united against him in order to cheat him in both the purchase and sale of goods, with the result that he found himself in debt, and in prison.

At this point, his former acquaintance, Miss Matthews, enters his life again. Their adulterous relationship causes Booth great anguish, but he is unable to mount sufficient resolution to end it. Fielding explains: "Repentance never failed to follow his transgressions; and yet so perverse is our judgment, and so slippery is the descent of vice when once we are entered into it, the same crime which he now repented of became a reason for doing that which was to cause his future repentance; and he continued to sin on because he had begun" (bk. 4, chap. 2).

Once released from prison, Booth fares little better, as he is able to deal neither with his friend Colonel James and the latter's interest in Miss Matthews, nor with Captain Trent, who lures him to the gambling table at the instigation of the dissolute peer. Particularly destructive is his lack of ethical standards that persuades him to attempt to bribe his way to military preferment. His final reduction to poverty results partly from his own actions, but also partly from circumstances beyond his ability and training to change. The absence of his counselor and friend, Dr. Harrison, combines with his own lack of education and training for other than a military career to prevent a successful adjustment to the changing circumstances of life.

The Story of Mrs. Bennet

A second illustration of the impoverishment of a basically good person is found in the story of Mrs. Bennet, whose fate is entangled with that of Booth and his family once they have settled in London. Her story occupies a large and important portion of the novel and must be dealt with as something more than a digressive tale. Mrs. Bennet is a significant factor in complicating the plot, as she warns Amelia of the danger she faces in dealing with the dissolute peer and as, to further her husband's career, she substitutes for Amelia at the masquerade.

Thematically, the tale of Mrs. Bennet and her first husband brings together many of the ingredients that led to the difficulties of Booth and Amelia. Malicious actions by relatives and acquaintances deprived Mrs. Bennet and her husband of an expected and deserved livelihood, and their efforts to stabilize their lives were marred by her husband's imprudence. Looming large in the story of Mrs. Bennet is her father's failure to provide, through education and training, for the eventuality that she might be forced to earn a living on her own. Her husband similarly fell victim to the incredulity of his uncle, who did not foresee that human dishonesty would act to frustrate his plans to establish his nephew in a living. Like Booth who was compelled to seek his living through military service, having been trained to no other trade or occupation, Mrs. Bennet's husband had to seek his sustenance in the Church, for which vocation his family had destined him. When opportunities to serve in either the army or the clergy are lacking, both men find adjustment to the realities of life difficult if not impossible.

Fielding stresses the importance of education as preparation for life, and he has a keen sense of the inadequacy of a merely classical training to provide a basis for earning a living. Education, important as it is, is not the whole story, however. Their husbands' imprudence and lack of sophistication in dealing with the world contribute substantially to the growing calamities of both Amelia and Mrs. Bennet.

Fielding's assertion, at the outset of *Amelia,* that we may account by natural means for the success of knaves and the calamities of fools because individuals lack prudence or follow blindly a predominant passion, is demonstrated in both cases. Mrs. Bennet is destroyed both by her father's errors of judgment and her own inability to react to altered conditions. When her father's wife and other child died, Mrs. Bennet became head of his household, a position that filled her with excusable pride and high expectations. As often happens, however, another woman entered her father's life, and Mrs. Bennet, innocently enough, could not forbear warning him against remarriage. Her own misguided efforts and those of a meddling aunt turned the good man and his new wife against her, and she was compelled to seek refuge with her aunt, who, learning that the young woman would receive only a scant inheritance from her father, coldly withdrew her support. Under these circumstances, Mrs. Bennet found attractive marriage to a neighboring young clergyman, who had similarly suffered from his father's imprudence. As in the case of Booth and Amelia, fortune was not alone responsible for their plight, but their own inadequate understanding of life and imprudent actions contributed to it. The Bennets could not be content with country life and were tempted by the allurements of wealth, or at least by the trappings of prosperity to be found in the city. This weighed heavily in their decision to try to set up their lives in London, deserting the modest cure they had obtained in the country, and subsequently led to Mrs. Bennet's involvement with the dissolute peer and the tragic events that followed.

Characterization in *Amelia*

Fielding's characterization of women often lacks sharp definition, and, unlike his portraits of men, his sense of female life seldom penetrates beyond the surface of their actions. Often, they seem to exist merely as foils to the evolution of the characters of the men with whom they interact in the fable. Neither Fanny Goodwill nor Sophia Western possesses an interesting personality. They are not memorable individuals although they possess many desirable traits. They have both moral understanding and strength of will. Both can act on their own initiatives in the absence of the men they love. Fanny uses her charms effectively in making Joseph's expression of his affections a comfortable and easy task. Sophia demonstrates strength of will and admirable sense and fortitude in her trip from the country to London, and she is mature in her responses to Tom's moral shortcomings. She leaves a trail for him to follow and succeeds in both pricking his conscience and whetting his desires. Neither heroine, however, makes a permanent impression on the reader's mind. Among lesser characters, such as Lady Booby, Mrs. Waters, and Lady Bellaston, all of whom have spicy roles in the novels, there is a similar lack of vividness, and, though they carry out their functions well, they are memorable mainly for their influence on Joseph or Tom, and not in themselves. Personalities like Mrs. Slipslop or Mrs. Western perform their often comic actions effectively but without distinction.

The title of Fielding's last novel, *Amelia,* gives promise of a fortuitous evolution of his treatment of women that is not fulfilled. Amelia herself, Mrs. Matthews, and the lesser figures of Mrs. Bennet and Mrs. Ellison provide interesting insights into the world of eighteenth-century women, without involving them in substantive action requiring moral choice. Like Mrs. Heartfree, Amelia is the ideal sentimental heroine whose actions can be predicted with a high degree of accuracy. Admirable as the loyalty of Booth's wife is, it adds little to the story in the way of dramatic conflict or real interest. While some suspense might have been created through the peer's pursuit of Amelia, Fielding dissipates this by providing her with prior warnings of his intentions. Here, as elsewhere, Amelia exists as a constant of connubial virtue, contrasting with the irresolute nature of Booth, and, in terms of the tradition of sentiment in which Fielding writes, the perfect virtue of Amelia combines with the moral strength Booth receives from his prison reading of Dr. Barrow to effect his reformation.

Miss Matthews interests the reader as an attractive personality possessed of shifting standards of virtue. Her conversations with Booth in prison and occasional remarks that convey much more to the reader than to Booth fix her as a passionate woman of the world. Mrs. Bennet is also of interest as a woman with human shortcomings but no truly heinous instincts. Although she is seduced much against her will by the peer, her ambition and vanity place her in a position from which her fall is almost certain. Her sprightly opportunism in taking advantage of Amelia's absence from the masquerade to advance her own interests contrasts refreshingly with the predictable perfection of Amelia. Mrs. Ellison also has interesting facets to her personality, and, although there is much that is reprehensible in her pimping for the peer, she is capable of acts of friendship within the framework of her admittedly amoral view of sexual conduct. Ultimately, however, what interest there is in the women in *Amelia* centers only on their involvement in the fate of Booth, and not on themselves as individuals.

Military characters appear frequently in *Amelia,* developing an interest Fielding had tangentially begun in *Tom Jones.* Tom is tempted to follow the military to join the war against Prince Charles after he meets Partridge, and it is only a series of accidents culminating in the appearance of Sophia that diverts him to London. The military mentality, through the threat of dueling, continues its presence in Tom's involvement with Mr. Fitzpatrick and with Ensign Northerton. In *Amelia* the cast of military characters is appropriately larger, for Booth has spent a substantial part of his early marriage as an officer at Gibraltar. Colonel James, Colonel Bath, Sergeant Atkinson, and Captain Trent are all military acquaintances whose past associations influence their relationship with Booth.

Sergeant Atkinson, Booth's loyal friend, echoes the loyal servant of the sentimental tradition. By far the least attractive of the military figures is Captain Trent, who is employed by the dissolute peer to destroy Booth. His life does little credit to the military, and he makes a living, when not employed by the peer, by pimping for his wife, who in turn supports him through prostitution.

Colonel James is the most interesting of the military personalities. He is a sincere friend of Booth, but their relationship is strained when he mistakenly assumes that Booth shares his interest in Miss Matthews, and Booth narrowly misses dueling with him on that account. Their brief conflict does in fact involve Booth in a duel with Colonel Bath, whose mind dwells constantly on violence and particularly on the need for fighting to satisfy matters of honor. Bath is the brother-in-law of James, and his sensitivity to the latter's honor compels him to goad Booth into a duel which Booth wins by running the colonel through, miraculously without inflicting substantial injury. Bath's excessive sense of honor and dedication to seeing that others live up to his artificially created code of behavior borders on comedy, but in reality flirts with tragedy.

As a group, Fielding's military characters represent a cross section of those trained to that vocation, but with very little interest to the reader beyond that traditionally associated with the comradeship of arms: friendship, sex, and dueling.

The introduction of Dr. Harrison returns to one of Fielding's familiar concerns: the clergy and their importance in setting the moral tone of English society. Dr. Harrison appears early and furthers Booth's relationship with Amelia, helping them to marry and assisting them on many subsequent occasions. The presence of Dr. Harrison helps, moreover, to advance Fielding's analysis of Booth's religious views, views which Amelia does not share and which give her "great uneasiness" because they suggest to her that he is "little better than an atheist" (bk. 10, chap. 9). It is only his own good nature that prompts Booth to treat his neighbors with charity, and his actions emanate from a personal sense of what is right rather than from religious principles. The result, as is frequently demonstrated in the novel, is a failure to make proper discriminations and an inability to resist the temptations of the moment.

Booth's ideas are not without some merit in terms of common experience. He suggests to Amelia, during a discussion of the cruelty of men of position and power, that "Compassion, if thoroughly examined, will, I believe, appear to be the fellow-feeling only of men of the same rank and degree of life for one another, on account of the evils to which they themselves are liable. Our sensations are, I am afraid, very cold towards those who are at a great distance from us, and whose calamities can consequently never reach us" (bk. 10, chap. 9). These are the words of an acute observer of human conduct but are not shared by Amelia, who has been greatly influenced by the benevolence of Dr. Harrison as well as by his philosophy. Amelia recalls Dr. Harrison's quotation from "some Latin book": "I am a man myself, and my heart is interested in whatever can befall the rest of mankind." Amelia adds her own commentary to it: "That is the sentiment of a good man, and whoever thinks otherwise is a bad one" (bk. 10, chap. 9). In most of his actions Booth could meet Amelia's expectations of what a good man should be, but through natural instinct and not conviction. His views are determined by his belief that all men act under the influence of a predominant passion and from a principle of self-love: "Where benevolence therefore is the uppermost passion, self-love directs you to gratify it by doing good, and by relieving the distresses of others; for they are then in reality your own. But where ambition, avarice, pride, or any other passion, governs the man and keeps his benevolence down, the miseries of all other men affect him no more than they would a stock or a stone" (bk. 10, chap. 9).

Earlier in the novel Dr. Harrison had discussed this subject in response to Amelia's disillusionment over the villainy of mankind: "The nature of man is far from being in itself evil; it abounds with benevolence, charity, and pity, coveting praise and honour, and shunning shame and disgrace. Bad education, bad habits, and bad customs debauch our nature, and drive it headlong as it were into vice" (bk. 9, chap. 5). Dr. Harrison is in the tradition of Shaftesbury whose vision of mankind is essentially optimistic, contrasting with the more pessimistic appraisal of human nature nurtured by Hobbes and his followers, and seen in the eighteenth century in the cynicism of Mandeville's suggestion that private vice is, in the final analysis, a public benefit. Fielding clearly leans toward the optimism of Shaftesbury, but it is not without a robust and penetrating analysis of how human nature has been corrupted by the pressures of society, especially those resulting from shortcomings in education and religious training. While a supporter of the institution of the clergy, and capable of offering the reader portraits of fine representatives of that class, such as the quixotic Parson Adams or eminently charitable Dr. Harrison, Fielding recognizes that the clergy more often than not fall short of the ideal that he sets for them, and that the same goals of material prosperity and the emoluments of position that motivate society in general move the clergy to concentrate more on preferment than on the instruction of the faithful.

Dr. Harrison is a major factor in the novel, as *Amelia* draws to its conclusion, both as a catalyst in the plot and as a yardstick by which the moral actions and ideas of the principal characters can be judged. In a material way, the revelation that Amelia is the true heir to the family fortune leaves the reader with every expectation that prosperity will greet the young couple and their family. The more essential threat to their future happiness, however, is the wavering moral attitudes of Booth, and his belief that men act from a predominant passion. He is, moreover, subject to pride and to imprudence to such a degree that the acquisition of a fortune would likely lead to its dissipation. Booth needs moral strengthening, and his association with Dr. Harrison alone has not provided it. When he is imprisoned, however, he takes up the reading of Dr. Barrow's writings in quiet moments and is converted to Christianity. Booth describes the mechanics of his conversion to Dr. Harrison when the clergyman visits him in prison: "Since I have been in this wretched place," he tells his learned friend, "I have employed my time almost entirely in reading over a series of sermons which are contained in that book (meaning Dr. Barrow's works, which then lay on the table before him) in proof of the Christian religion; and so good an effect have they had upon me, that I shall, I believe, be the better man for them as long as I live. I have not a doubt (for I own I have had such) which remains now unsatisfied." To Dr. Harrison's expression of the hope that the experience will influence his future life, he adds, "I need not tell you, sir, that will always be the case where faith is sincere, as I assure you mine is. Indeed, I never was a rash disbeliever; my chief doubt was founded on this—that as men appeared to me to act entirely from their passions, their actions could have neither merit nor demerit" (bk. 12, chap. 5). Booth is thus prepared to undertake, with Amelia, the responsibilities of married life.

One last principle of living remains for the novelist to clarify before ending the story of Booth and Amelia. What would have happened if fate had not provided Amelia with a fortune? After Booth has learned of the dishonesty of Murphy and Amelia's sister in forging their mother's will, and now knows that his wife has inherited a fortune, he temporarily withholds the information in order to test her. Released from prison and at home, Booth learns from Amelia that Atkinson and his wife have offered them twenty pounds if it would help them in their distress, and he pretends to want to accept it. His wife would rather not take charity from those who need it as much as she does, and the situation develops into a discussion of poverty, charity, and how best to live. To Booth's question, "How then shall we live?" Amelia unhesitatingly replies, "By our labour." To the further question concerning whether or not she could really support such a life, she responds: "I am sure I could be happy in it," and adds, "And why not I as well as a thousand others, who have not the happiness of such a husband to make life delicious? why should I complain of my hard fate while so many who are much poorer than I enjoy theirs? Am I of a superior rank of being to the wife of the honest labourer? am I not partaker of one common nature with her?" (bk. 12, chap. 8).

Amelia, thus prepared to accept life as a poor woman, is able to accept the responsibilities of having a fortune, for she understands the needs of the poor and reflects, somewhat ahead of her time, an understanding of the dignity of labor. Fielding thus modifies the sentimental tradition that he had inherited largely from the theater and with which he frequently flirts in his novels, for in *Amelia* the conversion of Booth is not achieved merely or even primarily through the virtuous example of his beloved, but through religious conversion. The Christian principles that Booth now espouses he finds echoed in the sentiments of Amelia. His is no fifth-act repentance that will be subject to a relapse, but it is firmly rooted in his intellectual and moral rejuvenation that is the result of religious strength. His test of Amelia is demonstration of the independence of his thought, and he is prepared to actively direct their fortunes.

Fielding's final achievement in prose fiction is drawn in dark colors, and there is little of the lightness that characterized what has been called "the feast of life" in *Tom Jones*. Life, however, does not end with the marriage of two lovers, and the pressures on Amelia and Booth are far greater after marriage than before. Tom Jones learns much about life and experiences a maturation that recognizes the beauty and virtue of Sophia. This makes it unlikely that he will suffer such lapses in conduct as he did with Molly Seagrim or Mrs. Waters because the overwhelming beauty and charm of his beloved have fortified his naturally good instincts toward benevolence and virtue. Such a sentimental view of life seldom suffices, however, and Fielding's sense of the beauty of existence amid the cruelty and confusions of life required a further statement than that found in *Tom Jones*. In *Amelia* he suggests that the less ebullient aspects of existence often associated with religion and faith are needed if Booth is to reform his life by solving the mystery inherent in the relationship between passion and conduct. Although Fielding's last novel is less cheerful than its immediate predecessor, it is a profound and often brilliant commentary on human life that is intellectually satisfying.

Chapter Six

Energy to the Last

The Journal of a Voyage to Lisbon

The last years of Fielding's life were devoted largely to public service in an effort to reduce the level of violent crime in London. His preoccupation with crime and criminals is evident in his last novel, *Amelia,* and in the revision, at about the same time, of his earlier work on crime, *Jonathan Wild.* Although recognized as a satire on Robert Walpole, the English prime minister, when it was first published, the implications of the effect of master criminals such as Wild on honest and vulnerable members of society was demonstrated in the life of Heartfree and his family that takes up a large part of the work. Early in 1754 Fielding published his revision of the book as *The Life of Mr. Jonathan Wild the Great. A new Edition, with considerable Corrections and Additions.* The most significant change is the softening of the satire of the prime minister by shifting the emphasis of the irony so that it hits against politicians and great men in general. In these later years of his life Fielding had clearly softened his view of Walpole and, in *The Journal of a Voyage to Lisbon,* he refers to him as "one of the best of men and of ministers" (16:248).[1] The timing of the reissue of *Jonathan Wild* allows it and *Amelia* to support the social commentary developed in his *Proposal for the Poor,* his *Charge to the Grand Jury,* and his *Enquiry into the Late Increase of Robbers.* Moreover, in *A Clear State of the Case of Elizabeth Canning* (1753), he summarizes his involvement in the notorious case of a young woman who claimed to have been kidnapped, beaten, and abused, and who, after a long period of legal controversy accompanied by an extensive paper war among the pamphleteers, was convicted of perjury, possibly unjustly, and transported to the American colonies.

Physically broken by disease, but with his brilliant mind still acutely functioning, Fielding decided to undertake a sea voyage to Lisbon in the hope that the warmer climate would be beneficial to his health. Despite this last effort to preserve his life, Fielding was fully aware that he was dying, and the *Journal* is written with that fact clearly in mind. It forms the record of a passage that was expected to last no more than three weeks but that, in reality, took forty-three days because of initial delays and unfavorable winds. Meditating on these delays, Fielding finds occasion to reflect "how often the greatest abilities lie wind-bound as it were in life; or if they venture out, and attempt to beat the seas, they struggle in vain against wind and tide; and if they have not sufficient prudence to put back, are most probably cast away on the rocks and quicksands, which are every day ready to devour them" (272).

In the "Preface" to the *Voyage* Fielding demonstrates his continuing interest in a theory of writing and his sense of what can be accomplished in a particular genre. He is conscious that the recounter of voyages must be "an agreeable, as well as an instructive companion" (180) who will keep commentary to a minimum, supplying only that which his readers "could not possibly have obtained of themselves" (180). In his "Introduction" he looks back on the recent accomplishments of his life of service to the state, hoping that his efforts to reduce crime will merit a pension to provide for his family, since his failing health will prevent him from doing so himself. With a degree of honesty he declares: "And tho' I disclaim all pretence to that Spartan or Roman patriotism, which loved the public so well that it was always ready to become a voluntary sacrifice to the public good, I do solemnly declare I have that love for my family" (191). *The Journal of a Voyage to Lisbon* is, moreover, a work of considerable value in understanding the complex personality of the novelist and the factors that shaped his career and in its own right an interesting travel book that reveals a good deal about the difficulties experienced in undertaking a sea voyage during the eighteenth century.

Fielding's view of life expressed in his last published work possesses both the harsh perception of life and the compensating humanity that Smollett injects into the personality of Matthew Bramble in *Humphry Clinker*. An awareness of the selfishness, cruelty, and narrow self-concern of human nature dominates Fielding's thought. His vision, heightened by his own helplessness as he boards the ship, interprets passing the rows of sailors and watermen as running the gauntlet, as he notices that few fail "of paying their compliments . . . by all manner of insults and jests on my misery" (200). He understands life too well to consider such treatment directed against himself as an individual. "No man," he notes, "who knew me will think I conceived any personal resentment at this behaviour; but it was a lively picture of that cruelty and inhumanity, in the nature of men, which I have often contemplated with concern; and which leads the mind into a train of very uncomfortable and melancholy thoughts" (200–201). Fielding's ability to see the vicious aspect of human life in proper perspective indicates the source of his ability to write with great good humor in his novels without varnishing over any of the disagreeable facts of human existence. Even in these final days of life Fielding delights in the observation of reality that takes on, for him, a kind of beauty even in its most macabre expression.

The visit of two Customhouse officials provides an example of the kind of arrogance that is often sparked by the temporary power an individual enjoys in an official capacity. Fielding describes his measured response, and their consequent reaction. Having succeeded in having his visitors remove their hats in the presence of his wife, he finds that conciliatory efforts are met with a degree "of surliness" that convinces him that if he "should condescend to become more gentle, they would soon grow more rude" (214–15). He is similarly revolted by the greed of the people at the fishing village of Deal who take advantage of all who are becalmed nearby by charging exorbitant prices for whatever provisions they sell. "For these good people," he acidly suggests, "consider the sea as a large common, appendant to their manor, in which when they find any of their fellow creatures impounded, they conclude, that they have a full right of making them pay at their own discretion for their deliverance" (219–20).

Among the many men and women Fielding encounters on his voyage, clearly the individual who causes him the most annoyance is Mrs. Humphrys, at whose public house destiny forces him to make an extended visit. Mrs. Humphrys runs a house at which no luxury seems to exist but it has all the trappings of age and poverty that a miserly disposition rather than necessity can create. With her rotund and passive husband she preys on those individuals whom nature places in her path. Much of Fielding's skill in observation and use of satiric detail goes into her physical portrait: "A tyrant, a trickster, and a bully, generally wear the marks of their several dispositions in their countenances," Fielding tells us, adding that "so do the vixen, the shrew, the scold, and all other females of the like kind." Mrs. Humphrys is nature's example of all such creatures. "She was a short, squat woman; her head was closely joined to her shoulders, where it was fixed somewhat awry; every feature of her countenance was sharp and pointed; her face was furrowed with the small-pox; and her complexion, which seemed to be able to turn milk to curds, not a little resembled in colour such milk as had already undergone that operation" (236). Such details of appearance combined with a strident and scolding voice serve to both describe and characterize this ugly woman who never smiled and constantly complained about the charges she was able to levy on her customers: "If her bills were remonstrated against, she was not offended with the censure of her fair-dealing; if they were not, she seemed to regard it as a tacit sarcasm on her folly, which might have set down larger prices with the same success" (237).

Fielding's ability to use his sense of comedy to provide a biting commentary on the details of human existence is still strong, even in his last work. His vision, moreover, is not entirely jaundiced, and he can recognize goodness where it truly exists. Such is the case of the generous lady who inhabits a mansion in the vicinity of Mrs. Humphrys' house. Her disposition and character is quite the opposite of Fielding's hostess, and she is "not only extremely polite in her behaviour to strangers of her own rank, but so extremely good and charitable to all her poor neighbours, who stand in need of her assistance, that she hath the universal love and praises of all who live near her" (243). Fielding is even able to recognize the folly of his own suspicions in an incident in which he is ready to blame the dishonesty of his hostess for the loss of a treasured tea chest, only to find that it had been left quite innocently in the boat as preparations were being made to return to the ship. He relates this story, in which the jest is on him, with unvarnished accuracy and good humor.

Fielding's continuing quarrel with Mrs. Humphrys does not obscure his ability to recognize the true beauty of the surrounding countryside. Moreover, despite the difficulty experienced in obtaining suitable food, he and his party find their greatest enjoyment in the good fellowship generated at mealtime. The novelist's account of his adventures leads him to reflect on social concerns that were preoccupying him during the years preceding his voyage, the effect of the "mob" on society, the problem of putting the poor to work, and ways to confront the selfishness and lack of charity of people in general.

Fielding describes the village surrounding the farm of Mrs. Humphrys in appreciative terms:

This pleasant village is situated on a gentle ascent from the water, whence it affords that charming prospect I have above described. Its soil is gravel, which assisted with its declivity, preserves it always so dry, that immediately after the most violent rain, a fine lady may walk without wetting her silken shoes. The fertility of the place is apparent from its extraordinary verdure, and it is so shaded with large and flourishing elms, that its narrow lanes are a natural grove or walk, which in the regularity of its plantation vies with the power of art, and its wanton exuberancy greatly exceeds it. (249)

Such a place only the perversity of human nature could destroy, but the petulant selfishness and miserly greed of Mrs. Humphrys does not allow the beauty of the surrounding country to soften her attitude toward people and things. Not that Fielding's vision is to be entirely trusted. He sees little value in the extreme cleanliness with which his hostess prepares for his visit, and which she places before graciousness and warmth in her hierarchy of values. Her portrait and that of her husband provide a context for the expression of Fielding's last commentary on a wide range of human activities. Among these is the pleasure of eating, which brings solace to the poor even as it does to those in ill health and the dying, such as himself. Despite his rapidly failing physical condition he had not lost his ability to eat and to enjoy food. Echoing a theme that he had often previously expressed, though perhaps most effectively in his description of the happy laughter of the poor eating their meal of one dish in the vision of Nehemiah Vinegar in the *Champion* (December 29, 1739), he calls attention to his own pleasure in eating in the company of close friends and relatives even in the unpleasant establishment of Mrs. Humphrys. Their first much-delayed meal is salvaged by the discovery of a fisherman living next door who supplies them with seals, whitings, and lobsters. "This discovery being made by accident, we completed the best, the pleasantest, and the merriest meal, with more appetite, more real, solid luxury, and more festivity, than was ever seen in an entertainment at White's" (229–30). Not only the food, but the sociability of eating is one of the great pleasures relished by Fielding, and nowhere more convincingly detailed than in his last *Journal*.

Fielding's pride in the British navy and in the nation's position as a great sea power is more strongly conveyed in the *Journal* than might be anticipated. He describes the shipyards of Deptford and Woolwich aᶜ noble sights, and justifies the building of the *Royal Anne,* the largest ship in the world, because it provides tangible evidence of England's superiority in naval affairs and, as such, will be an inspiration to seamen. He is impressed with the number and variety of ships. "Besides the ships in the docks, we saw many on the water: the yachts are sights of great parade, and the king's body yacht is, I believe, unequalled in any country, for convenience as well as magnificence; . . ." (210). Moreover, the whole scene, in its variety and extent "forms a most pleasing object to the eye, as well as highly warming to the heart of an Englishman, who has any degree of love for his country, or can recognize any effect of the patriot in his constitution" (210). Fielding is proud of his country not only for its naval might but also for the evidence of national charity that is apparent in the Royal Hospital of Greenwich that overlooks the water and forms a sight that "doth such honour at once to its builder and the nation, to the great skill and ingenuity of the one, and to the no less sensible gratitude of the other. . . ." (210). Fielding's enthusiasm for such tangible reflections of the highest ideals and aspirations of his nation contrasts with and counterbalances his acid commentary on the petty and narrow attitudes of individual citizens. In addition, he is surprisingly capable of appreciating the glories of nature, although his enjoyment is often accompanied by serious reflection. In the midst of a calm at sea his party watches the magnificence of the sunset from the deck of their ship and the eloquence of Fielding's description in worth transcribing:

We were seated on the deck, women and all, in the serenest evening that can be imagined. Not a single cloud presented itself to our view, and the sun himself was the only object which engrossed our whole attention. He did indeed set with a majesty which is incapable of description, with which, while the horizon was yet blazing with glory, our eyes were called off to the opposite part to survey the moon, which was then at full, and which in rising presented us with the second object that this world hath offered to our vision. Compared to these the pageantry of theatres, or splendor of courts, are sights almost below the regard of children. (276)

Fielding's *Journal of a Voyage to Lisbon* is not a happy book in the sense that it reflects the kind of exuberance that characterized *Tom Jones*. The prospect of death and the necessity of providing for the welfare of his family is a constant preoccupation with the novelist, and the acidity with which he expresses his ideas may in some respects at least be traceable to his physical discomfort and incapacity. On the other hand, his constant concern for his wife and his sense of the continuing needs of humanity provide strong evidence of the selflessness of Fielding's spirit and the genuine resignation he felt toward the inevitability of death as part of the common destiny of man.

Response to the publication of the *Journal* was generally polite if unenthusiastic. Fielding's involvement in the case of Elizabeth Canning had given his critics a rare opportunity to press their attack against him. But the *Journal of a Voyage to Lisbon* was a different sort of book, entirely devoid of political overtones and uninvolved in the specifics of London life. Horace Walpole treated it roughly and some of Richardson's devotees adversely criticized it, but most critics, such as those in the *London*

Magazine, the *Monthly Review,* and the *Gentleman's Magazine,* found it worthy of praise. Only a reader who fails to understand the method and value of satire could find general fault with the treatment of Mr. and Mrs. Humphrys, who ultimately emerge as representative types of the broad range of selfishness inherent in humanity. They are sufficiently obscure as individuals that the personal aspects of their portraits are lost in the more universal significance that they have. More questionable might be the treatment of the captain of the ship on which Fielding sailed. The continuing jest about the captain's observations concerning the wind, and some incidents in which Fielding quarrels with him portray the seaman in an unfavorable light, but there is little that is vicious or harmful. The possibility that some offense might have been taken is suggested by the appearance of two different versions of the *Journal* in 1755, one of which was considerably shortened and altered by the omission of a number of details concerning the captain, and by the removal of language that might have reflected unfavorably on either Fielding himself or close friends or associates. The shorter version seems to have been published first, but the longer one was adopted by Arthur Murphy for his edition of Fielding's works. Henley chose to use the shorter version, while supplying most of the missing material in his notes.[2] Neither version is truly offensive, however, in the light of the satiric tone and acidly humorous pose assumed by Fielding throughout the work.

Fielding died shortly after landing at Lisbon, and the *Journal* is the last literary work to come from his pen. What it reveals about his character is in no way inconsistent with the manner in which he conducted his life. His sense of a Christianity that demands that the individual translate a benevolent view of his fellowman into daily action is still dominant and buttressed by an unrelenting sense of how habitually most human beings fall short of that ideal. Perhaps more clearly than in most of his previous works, his affection for England comes through to reinforce the sociological thrust of much of his earlier work. Most important to note, his skill as a writer is still with him, and Fielding's last work has vitality and interest as a work of art beyond its fascination for the reader as an autobiographical document.

Notes and References

Chapter One

1. William Congreve, *Love for Love,* London, 1695.
2. William Congreve, *The Way of the World,* London, 1700.
3. Samuel Johnson (of Cheshire), *Hurlothrumbo; or the Super-Natural.* London, 1729.
4. Nathaniel Lee, *The Rival Queens,* London, 1677; John Banks, *The Albion Queens,* altered from *The Island Queens,* London, 1684; James Thomson, *The Tragedy of Sophonisba,* London, 1730.
5. John Dryden, *All for Love,* London, 1678, act 3, sc. 1, 417 ff.
6. *The Fall of Mortimer,* London, 1731. Anonymous, but attributed to William Hatchett.
7. *The Complete Works of Henry Fielding,* ed. Henley, 11:173–74.
8. Ibid., p. 195.

Chapter Two

1. George Villiers, *The Rehearsal,* London, 1672.
2. John Dryden, *The Conquest of Granada,* London, 1672.
3. Fielding, *A Proposal for Making an Effectual Provision for the Poor,* London, 1753; Daniel Defoe, *Giving Alms No Charity, and Employing the Poor a Grievance to the Nation,* London, 1704.
4. *The Complete Works of Henry Fielding,* ed. Henley, 13:141.
5. Ibid., 13:171.
6. Ibid., 16:248.
7. Ibid., 14:75.
8. Ibid., 14:282.

Chapter Three

1. Although regular drama was limited to the two patent theaters, other kinds of entertainment were permitted at other playhouses, particularly performances including music, such as pantomimes and puppet shows.
2. The definitive attribution of the authorship of *Shamela* to Fielding was not made until the twentieth century, and the work is not included in the Henley edition. See Charles B. Woods, "Fielding and the Authorship of *Shamela,*" *Philological Quarterly* 25 (1946):248–72; and *An Apology for the Life of Mrs.*

Shamela Andrews, ed. with Introduction and Notes by Sheridan Baker (Berkeley and Los Angeles: University of California Press, 1953).

3. For a discussion of the imitations and parodies of *Pamela,* see F. Homes Dudden, *Henry Fielding* (Oxford, 1952), 1:313–15; and Bernard Kreissman, *Pamela-Shamela: A Study of the Criticisms, Burlesques, Parodies, and Adaptations of Richardson's "Pamela"* (Lincoln, Neb., 1960), pp. 7–22.

4. Dudden, *Henry Fielding,* 1:324.

5. On Fielding's creation of a prose epic much has been written, including Ethel Thornbury, *Henry Fielding's Theory of the Comic Prose Epic* (Madison, Wisc., 1931); E. M. W. Tillyard, *The Epic Strain in the English Novel* (New York, 1958); Ian Watt, "Fielding and the Epic Theory of the Novel," in *The Rise of the Novel: Studies in Defoe, Richardson and Fielding* (Berkeley and Los Angeles, 1957); and J. Paul Hunter, *Occasional Form: Henry Fielding and the Chains of Circumstance* (Baltimore, 1975).

6. On digressions in *Joseph Andrews,* see I. B. Cauthen, Jr., "Fielding's Digressions in *Joseph Andrews,*" *College English* 17 (1956):379–82.

7. Alexander Pope, *Epistle to Dr. Arbuthnot,* London, 1734, l. 306.

8. Henry Fielding, *Covent Garden Journal,* Tuesday, January 28, and Saturday, February 1, 1752.

9. Dudden, *Henry Fielding,* 1:432.

Chapter Four

1. Dudden, *Henry Fielding,* 1:388; 2:721–4, 879–80.

2. Dudden, *Fielding,* 2:676.

3. For a detailed study of the plot of the novel, see R. S. Crane, "The Plot of *Tom Jones,*" *Journal of General Education* 4 (1950):112–30.

4. There have been numerous new approaches to a study of the structure of *Tom Jones,* important among them, Robert V. Wess, "The Probable and Marvelous in *Tom Jones,*" *Modern Philology* 68 (1970):32–45; Aubrey Williams, "Interpositions of Providence and the Design of Fielding's Novels," *South Atlantic Quarterly* 70 (1971):256–86; and Henry Knight Miller, *Henry Fielding's "Tom Jones" and the Romance Tradition* (Victoria, 1976).

5. Of considerable interest is the wedding of epic and romance traditions in Miller's study of the romance tradition.

Chapter Five

1. In conjunction with *Amelia,* Fielding's social pamphlets are important. See Malvin R. Zirker, *Fielding's Social Pamphlets* (Berkeley, 1966).

2. On the way Fielding adapts the *Aeneid,* see Lyall H. Powers, "The Influence of the *Aeneid* on Fielding's *Amelia,*" *Modern Language Notes* 71 (1956):330–36.

Chapter Six

1. *The Works of Henry Fielding,* ed. Henley, 16. References in the text are by page number in this volume.

2. Ibid., pp. 285–308 *passim.*

Selected Bibliography

PRIMARY SOURCES

An Apology for the Life of Mrs. Shamela Andrews. Edited with Introduction and Notes by Sheridan Baker. Berkeley and Los Angeles: University of California Press, 1953.

An Apology for the Life of Mrs. Shamela Andrews, 1741. Augustan Reprint Society Publication #57. Los Angeles: Clark Memorial Library, 1956. A facsimile reprint with an Introduction by Ian Watt.

The Complete Works of Henry Fielding, with an Essay on the Life, Genius and Achievements of the Author. Edited by Ernest William Henley. 16 vols. New York: Croscup and Sterling, 1903. Reprinted, New York: Barnes and Noble, 1967. This is the most complete edition currently available.

The Regents Restoration Drama Series. Lincoln: University of Nebraska Press. This series contains a number of Fielding's plays with the following available: *The Author's Farce.* Edited by Charles B. Woods, 1966. *The Grub-Street Opera.* Edited by Edgar V. Roberts, 1968. *The Historical Register* and *Euridice Hissed.* Edited by William Appleton, 1967.

The Wesleyan Edition of the Works of Henry Fielding. Middletown, Conn.: Wesleyan University Press, and Oxford: Clarendon Press. This edition is in progress with the following volumes available: *The Jacobite's Journal and Related Writings.* Edited by W. B. Coley, 1975. *Joseph Andrews.* Edited by Martin Battestin, 1967. *Tom Jones.* Edited by Fredson Bowers, 1975.

SECONDARY SOURCES

Alter, Robert. *Fielding and the Nature of the Novel.* Cambridge: Harvard University Press, 1968. An important reconsideration of Fielding, offering valuable critical insights, particularly on *Amelia.*

Amory, Hugh. "Henry Fielding and the Criminal Legislation of 1751–2." *Philological Quarterly* 50 (1971):175–92. Discusses the connection between Fielding's efforts to reform criminal law and the activities of Parliament at the time.

Anderson, Howard. "Answers to the Author of *Clarissa:* Theme and Narrative Technique in *Tom Jones* and *Tristram Shandy.*" *Philological Quarterly* 51 (1972): 859–73. Argues that *Tom Jones* and *Tristram Shandy* establish through narrative techniques the possibility and necessity of mutual trust on the part of the main characters of the novels, rather than the self-reliance of Richardson's heroines.

Baker, Sheridan. "Fielding's *Amelia* and the Materials of Romance." *Philological Quarterly* 41 (1962): 437–49. The tradition of romance and emergence of sentiment in *Amelia*.

————."Political Allusion in Fielding's *Author's Farce, Mock Doctor,* and *Tumble-Down Dick,*" *PMLA* 77 (1962): 221–31. Examination of Fielding's anti-Walpole satire.

Bateson, F. W. "Henry Fielding." In *English Comic Drama, 1700–1750,* pp. 115–43. New York and Oxford: Clarendon Press, 1929. Fielding's mastery of contemporary realism in comedy, farce, and burlesque.

Battestin, Martin. *The Moral Basis of Fielding's Art: A Study of Joseph Andrews.* Middletown, Conn.: Wesleyan University Press, 1959. A significant study of the moral and religious ideas that inform *Joseph Andrews* as a Christian epic.

————."Tom Jones and 'His *Egyptian* Majesty': Fielding's Parable of Government." *PMLA* 82 (1967): 68–77. The incident in book 12, chapter 11 of the novel, in which Tom Jones and Partridge encounter a band of gypsies, is used as the basis for a discussion of Fielding's mastery of analogy, allusion, and symbol.

————."Fielding's Definition of Wisdom: Some Functions of Ambiguity as Emblem in *Tom Jones.*" *English Literary History* 25 (1968): 188–217. Fielding's development of his concept of *wisdom* through his use of artistic devices.

————, ed. *Twentieth Century Interpretations of "Tom Jones."* Englewood Cliffs, N.J.: Prentice Hall, 1968. A collection of important modern studies of *Tom Jones.*

Blanchard, Frederic T. *Fielding the Novelist: A Study of the Novelist's Fame and Influence.* New Haven: Yale University Press, 1926. A consideration of Fielding's reputation in relation to that of Richardson.

Bloch, Tuvia. "*Amelia* and Booth's Doctrine of the Passions." *Studies in English Literature* 13 (1973): 461–73. Suggests that Fielding shares Booth's view of the passions as determinants of action.

Booth, Wayne C. "The Self-Conscious Narrator in Comic Fiction before *Tristram Shandy.*" *PMLA* 67 (1952): 163–85. A discussion of the first-person narrator before Sterne, with an important section devoted to Fielding.

Butt, John. *Fielding,* Writers and their Work, #57. London: Longmans Green, 1954. Revised, 1959. A good brief study of Fielding.

Cauthen, I. B. "Fielding's Digressions in *Joseph Andrews.*" *College English* 17 (1956): 379–82. Argues the suitability of Fielding's digressions as related to his aesthetic of the novel.

Coley, William B. "The Background of Fielding's Laughter." *Journal of English Literary History* 26 (1959): 229–52. The influence of South, Shaftesbury, and Swift on Fielding's sense of the comic.

Cooke, Arthur L. "Henry Fielding and the Writers of Heroic Romance." *PMLA* 62 (1947): 984–94. Fielding's theory of the comic prose epic and that of Mlle. de Scudéry.

Crane, R. S. "The Plot of *Tom Jones.*" *Journal of General Education* 4 (1950): 112–30. A detailed discussion of the plot of the novel as a means of fusing character, action, and thought.

Cross, Wilbur L. *The History of Henry Fielding.* 3 vols. New Haven: Yale University Press, 1918. The standard biography.

Digeon, Aurelien. *The Novels of Fielding.* London: Routledge & Kegan Paul, 1925. An excellent general introduction to Fielding.

Dircks, Richard J. "The Perils of Heartfree: A Sociological Review of Fielding's Adaptation of Dramatic Convention." *Texas Studies in Literature and Language* 8 (1966): 5–13. The Heartfree episode as Fielding's device for focusing on the social impact of the criminal on society.

Dudden, F. Homes. *Henry Fielding: His Life, Works and Times.* 2 vols. Oxford: Clarendon Press, 1952. Provides a more detailed discussion of individual works than does Cross and includes much helpful background material.

Dyson, A. E. "Satiric and Comic Theory in Relation to Fielding." *Modern Language Quarterly* 18 (1957): 225–37. Distinguishes between satire and comedy in terms of how they judge man. Sees Fielding's work as primarily comic since it judges man against an ethical rather than an ideal norm.

Evans, James E. "Fielding, *The Whole Duty of Man, Shamela,* and *Joseph Andrews.*" *Philological Quarterly* 61 (1982): 212–19. Use of *The Whole Duty of Man* as a refutation of the tenets of Methodism and supportive of Fielding's own ethical views.

Farrell, William J. "The Mock-Heroic Form of *Jonathan Wild.*" *Modern Philology* 63 (1965): 216–26. Maintains that Fielding employs the traditional form used in the biography of illustrious people to satirize Wild in a mock-heroic manner.

Goggin, L. P. "Development of Techniques in Fielding's Comedies." *PMLA* 67 (1952): 769–81. Emphasizes Fielding's accomplishment in the comedy of manners.

Goldberg, Homer. "Comic Prose Epic or Comic Romance: The Argument of the Preface to *Joseph Andrews.*" *Philological Quarterly* 43 (1964): 193–215. Considers Fielding's term "comic epic in prose" and the reasoning in the Preface to *Joseph Andrews* as modeled on Aristotle's *Poetics.*

———. *The Art of Joseph Andrews*. Chicago: University of Chicago Press, 1969. A study of the relationship of the structure of the novel to its ethical concerns and comic intention, through a comparison with *Don Quixote, Le Roman comique, Gil Blas, Marianne,* and *Le Paysan parvenu*.

Golden, Morris. *Fielding's Moral Psychology*. Amherst: University of Massachusetts Press, 1966. Fielding's moral and social attitudes as they influence characterization in the novels.

Goldgar, Bertrand A. "The Politics of Fielding's *Coffee House Politician*." *Philological Quarterly* 49 (1970): 424–29. Examines the parallel between the Charteris case of 1730 and Fielding's *The Coffee House Politician*.

Goldknopf, David. "The Failure of Plot in *Tom Jones*." *Criticism* 11 (1969): 262–74. Considers the introductory chapters in *Tom Jones* as of little aesthetic value and points to a weakness in plot structure.

Grundy, Isobel M. "New Verse by Henry Fielding." *PMLA* 87 (1972): 213–45. Examines recently discovered verse by Fielding and considers how it might have been composed to please Lady Mary Wortley Montagu.

Hahn, H. George. *Henry Fielding: An Annotated Bibliography*. Metuchen, N.J.: Scarecrow, 1979. A valuable research aid.

Hatfield, Glen W. "Puffs and Politricks: *Jonathan Wild* and the Political Corruption of Language." *Philological Quarterly* 46 (1967): 248–67. The corruption of language by politicians as an object of Fielding's satire, particularly in *Jonathan Wild*.

Humphreys, A. R. ed. *Jonathan Wild* and *The Journal of a Voyage to Lisbon*. London: Dent. 1973. Introduction by Humphreys.

Hunter, J. Paul. *Occasional Form: Henry Fielding and the Chains of Circumstance*. Baltimore: Johns Hopkins University Press, 1975. Argues that Fielding is writing in the epic tradition.

Hutchens, Eleanor N. *Irony in "Tom Jones."* University: University of Alabama Press, 1965. A study of Fielding's oblique verbal irony.

Irwin, Michael. *Henry Fielding: The Tentative Realist*. Oxford: Clarendon Press, 1967. Argues that Fielding's primary concern in his novels is always didactic.

Irwin, W. R. *The Making of "Jonathan Wild": A Study in the Literary Method of Henry Fielding*. New York: Columbia University Press, 1941. Through a study of sources, examines *Jonathan Wild* as a mock epic.

———. "Satire and Comedy in the Works of Henry Fielding." *English Literary History* 13 (1946): 168–88. Fielding's theory of the comic prose epic as a means of coordinating the subjects of his satiric attacks.

Johnson, Maurice. *Fielding's Art of Fiction*. Philadelphia: University of Pennsylvania Press, 1961. A series of essays on Fielding's artistry in the novels, emphasizing his concern with fiction as a means of merging life and literature.

Kaplan, Fred. "Fielding's Novel about Novels: The 'Prefaces' and the 'Plot' of *Tom Jones.*" *Studies in English Literature* 13 (1973): 535–49. The importance of reading the "Prefaces" in *Tom Jones* to a study of the novel.

Kermode, Frank. "Richardson and Fielding." *Cambridge Journal* 4 (1950): 106–14. A study of the disparity between action and character in Fielding's heroes, and a justification of Richardson.

Kreisman, Bernard. *Pamela-Shamela: A Study of the Criticisms, Burlesques, Parodies, and Adaptations of Richardson's "Pamela."* Lincoln: University of Nebraska Press, 1960, pp. 7–22. *Shamela* and *Joseph Andrews* in the light of eighteenth-century reactions to *Pamela*.

Kropf, Carl R. "Educational Theory and Human Nature in Fielding's Works." *PMLA* 89 (1974): 113–20. Examines Fielding's idea of character and his belief that it may be influenced by birth and education.

Lockwood, Thomas. "A New Essay by Fielding." *Modern Philology* 78 (1980): 48–58. Argues for Fielding's authorship of an anonymous article.

Loftis, John. *Comedy and Satire from Congreve to Fielding.* Stanford: Stanford University Press, 1950, pp. 114–21. A study of the social background to Fielding's plays.

Longmire, Samuel E. "Allworthy and Barrow: The standards for Good Judgment." *Texas Studies in Literature and Language* 13 (1972): 629–39. A study of the mistaken judgments of Allworthy in *Tom Jones* as seen by reader and author.

Lutwack, Leonard. "Mixed and Uniform Prose Styles in the Novel." *Journal of Aesthetics and Art Criticism* 18 (1960): 350–57. Considers how the choice of a mixed or uniform style affects plot structure.

McCrea, Brian. *Henry Fielding and the Politics of Mid-Eighteenth Century England.* Athens: University of Georgia Press, 1981. Fielding's political writings, stressing his whig leanings.

McKillop, A. D. *"Henry Fielding."* In *The Early Masters of English Fiction,* pp. 98–146. Lawrence: University of Kansas Press, 1956. Valuable treatment of the novels.

Mandel, Jerome. "The Man of the Hill and Mrs. Fitzpatrick: Character and Narrative Technique in *Tom Jones.*" *Papers on Language and Literature* 5 (1969): 26–38. Suggests that the two digressive tales parody narrative technique and that both tales are relevant to the structure of *Tom Jones.*

Miller, Henry Knight. "The Digressive Tales in Fielding's *Tom Jones* and the Perspective of Romance." *Philological Quarterly* 54 (1975): 258–74. Relates the digressive tales to the romance tradition: The Man of the Hill is the literary descendant of the pius hermit of that tradition, while Mrs. Fitzpatrick deliberately runs counter to it.

———. *Essays on Fielding's "Miscellanies": A Commentary on Volume I.* Princeton, N.J.: Princeton University Press, 1961. An important commentary on the first volume of the *Miscellanies.*

————. *Henry Fielding's "Tom Jones" and the Romance Tradition.* English Literary Studies, #6. Victoria: University of Victoria Press, 1976. A suggestive and thorough treatment of the romance tradition as applied to *Tom Jones.*

Morrissey, L. J. *Henry Fielding: A Reference Guide.* Boston: G. K. Hall, 1980. A useful research tool.

Paulson, Ronald. *Fielding: A Collection of Critical Essays.* Englewood Cliffs, N.J.: Prentice Hall, 1962. A well-selected group of essays on Fielding. Contains a good annotated bibliography.

————. "Fielding in *Tom Jones:* The Historian, the Poet, and the Mythologist." In J. C. Hilson, M. M. B. Jones, and J. R. Watson, eds., *Augustan Worlds: New Essays in Eighteenth-Century Literature.* New York: Barnes and Noble, 1978. Fielding's multiple presence in the novel.

————. and Thomas Lockwood. *Henry Fielding: The Critical Heritage.* London: Routledge & Kegan Paul, 1969. Selected essays of critics from the time of Fielding to the late twentieth century.

————. *Satire and the Novel in Eighteenth-Century England.* New Haven: Yale University Press, 1967. A general study of satire in the novel with important comments on Fielding.

Powers, Lyall H. "The Influence of the *Aeneid* on Fielding's *Amelia.*" *Modern Language Notes* 71 (1956): 330–36. Compares *Amelia* with the *Aeneid* in terms of the number of books, characters, timing of action, and general structure.

Preston, John. *The Created Self: The Reader's Role in Eighteenth-Century Fiction.* London: Heineman, 1970. A study of how the novelist creates an audience for his work, with a section on Fielding.

Rawson, Claude J. "Fielding's 'Good' Merchant: the Problem of Heartfree in *Jonathan Wild.*" *Modern Philology* 69 (1972): 292–313. The moral and semantic differences of the words *good* and *great* as applied to Heartfree in *Jonathan Wild.*

————. *Henry Fielding and the Augustan Ideal under Stress.* Boston, Routledge & Kegan Paul, 1972. A group of separate essays that are individually and collectively valuable.

Rogers, Pat. *Henry Fielding: A Biography.* New York: Scribners, 1979. A short recent biography.

Rogers, Winfield H. "The Significance of Fielding's *Temple Beau.*" *PMLA* 55 (1940): 440–44. Fielding's use of humor characters.

Sacks, Sheldon. *Fiction and the Shape of Belief: A Study of Henry Fielding with Glances at Swift, Johnson, and Richardson.* Berkeley and Los Angeles: University of California Press, 1964. An inquiry into the relationship between ethical belief and literary form.

Schonhorn, Manuel. "Fielding's Digressive-Parodic Artistry: *Tom Jones* and the Man of the Hill." *Texas Studies in Literature and Language* 10 (1968): 207–14. Compares the digressive tale of The Man of the Hill to the tale of

Mr. Wilson in *Joseph Andrews*, to the facts of Tom's life, and to Virgil's *Aeneid*.

Sherburn, George. "Fielding's Social Outlook." *Philological Quarterly* 35 (1956): 1–23. The influence of moral philosophy on Fielding's spirit of reform.

Spacks, Patricia Meyer. "The Dangerous Age." *Eighteenth Century Studies* 11 (1977–78): 417–38. A study of adolescence in the novels of Fielding, Richardson, Goldsmith, Burney, and Smollett.

Spilka, Mark. "Fielding and the Epic Impulse." *Criticism* 11 (1969):68–77. Novelists since Fielding work on a larger scale than the traditional epic, responding to the expanding nature of social, political, and human concerns.

Stephanson, Raymond. "The Education of the Reader in Fielding's *Joseph Andrews*." *Philological Quarterly* 61 (1982):243–58. Manipulation of the reader as a means of educating him.

Stevick, Philip T. "Fielding and the Meaning of History." *PMLA* 79 (1964): 561–68. Fielding's sense of history as development.

Swann, George R. "Fielding and Empirical Realism." In *Philosophical Parallelism in Six English Novelists: The Conception of Good, Evil, and Human Nature*, pp. 46–64. Philadelphia: University of Pennsylvania Press, 1929. A consideration of the influence of Shaftesbury and Hume on Fielding's moral thought.

Taylor, Dick, Jr. "Joseph as Hero in *Joseph Andrews*." *Tulane Studies in English* 7 (1957): 91–109. Argues that Joseph Andrews matures in character in a way that is similar to the development of Tom Jones.

Thornbury, Ethel M. *Henry Fielding's Theory of the Comic Prose Epic*. Studies in Language and Literature, #30. Madison: University of Wisconsin Press, 1931. A background study of the epic as a basis for connecting *Joseph Andrews* and *Tom Jones* with that genre.

Tillyard, E. M. W. *The Epic Strain in the English Novel*. New York: Oxford University Press, 1958, pp. 510–58. Sees *Tom Jones* more as a romance than an epic.

Towers, A. R. "*Amelia* and the State of Matrimony." *Review of English Studies*, n.s., 5 (1954): 144–57. A study of marriage as a theme in the novel.

Watt, Ian. "Fielding and the Epic Theory of the Novel." In *The Rise of the Novel: Studies in Defoe, Richardson and Fielding*, pp. 239–59. Berkeley and Los Angeles: University of California Press, 1957. Suggests that although Fielding connects *Joseph Andrews* with the epic tradition, the novel is not an epic.

Wendt, Alan. "The Moral Allegory of *Jonathan Wild*." *English Literary History* 24 (1957): 306–20. On the ideas of goodness and greatness in *Jonathan Wild*, pointing toward an ideal that would combine the two.

————. "The Naked Virtue of Amelia." *English Literary History* 27 (1960): 131–48. A study of Amelia as a person.

Wess, Robert V. "The Probable and the Marvelous in *Tom Jones*." *Modern Philology* 68 (1970): 32–45. Examines the question of plausibility in the plot of *Tom Jones*.

Williams, Aubrey. "Interpositions of Providence and the Design of Fielding's Novels." *South Atlantic Quarterly* 70 (1971): 256–86. Considers Fielding's sense of the influence of providence on human affairs and its importance in shaping his plots.

Williams, Ioan. *The Criticism of Henry Fielding.* London: Routledge & Kegan Paul, 1970. A collection of Fielding's critical writings with an introduction.

Williams, Muriel B. *Marriage: Fielding's Mirror of Morality.* University: University of Alabama Press, 1973. Fielding's moral views, especially on marriage, are expressed through comedy.

Woods, Charles B. "Fielding and the Authorship of *Shamela*." *Philological Quarterly* 25 (1946): 248–72. The case for Fielding's authorship persuasively argued.

————. "The 'Miss Lucy' Plays of Fielding and Garrick." *Philological Quarterly* 41: 294–310. Argues that *Miss Lucy in Town* was co-authored by Fielding.

Work, James A. "Henry Fielding, Christian Censor." In *The Age of Johnson: Essays Presented to Chauncey Brewster Tinker.* Edited by F. W. Hilles, pp. 139–48. New Haven: Yale University Press, 1949. Suggests that traditional Christian morality is at the base of Fielding's work.

Wright, Andrew. *Henry Fielding: Mask and Feast.* Berkeley and Los Angeles: University of California Press, 1965. A useful theoretical study.

Zirker, Malvin R. *Fielding's Social Pamphlets: A study of "An Enquiry into the Causes of the Late Increase of Robbers" and "A Proposal for Making an Effectual Provision for the Poor."* Berkeley: University of California Press, 1966. An important study of Fielding's social writings that adds significant dimension to the thought of Fielding on the poor and crime developed in the novels.

Index